so many cannot integrate is such | helpful review of the German literature otherwise mores indexed in ritual studies

focus on Bell (Foucault

(rather than, say, the significance of Victor Turner for)

or

(Bourdieu purity + danger)

journeys stand for example by the Dutch Ritual Studies

FREE BOOK

liminality (ref)

post-Foucauldian 'strategy'

Negotiating Legitimacy

Rituals and Reflection in Schools

Robert Hamm

Negotiating Legitimacy

Rituals and Reflection in Schools

Published by Robert Hamm

Robert Hamm, 17 Meadow Vale, Sligo, Republic of Ireland

ISBN 978-0-9928271-0-6

Print: Lettertec Ireland Ltd., Carrigtohill, Co. Cork, Republic of Ireland

Contents

Thanks to all those who helped to get this book written:

Alexander, Alice, Anja, Anke, Anna, Anne, Ariane, Aurelien, Birgit, Candida, Carmel, Carmel, Celine, Christina, Claudia, Claudia, Deirdre, Dirk, Dirk, Engelbert, Franz, Frauke, Frigga, Gesine, Gusta, Hannah, Heike, Henriette, Henrik, Ida, Ina, Ines, Irene, Jana, Johanna, Jonas, John, John, Karen, Laurence, Leslie, Linda, Lisa, Marita, Marlies, Martin, Michael, Nicole, Rachel, Rebecca, Rebekka, Renate, Rosaline, Stephani, Suzanne, Svenja, Sylva, Sylvia,
and particularly

Tony Partridge

who went a long way from Russian philosophy to rituals in school.

Intro: Trying to Make Sense

My initial interest in rituals in education was triggered more than twenty-five years ago. When I was working as an educator in Germany I was often in a position where colleagues of mine would request from children that they form a line of pairs, that they come into line, that they stay in line. Looking at this practice I found that the reasons given by these colleagues for lining up the children often did not carry a lot of substance. The rationale given was usually that it was done for safety purposes. And yet, the arguments often made little sense.

The same children who are walking through Circular Road, Queens Avenue to Edward Street at 2 p.m. in a line of pairs, supervised to prevent damage of persons or goods are walking at 3 p.m. from Edward Street through Queens Avenue to Circular Road, unsupervised and not in a line of pairs, on their way home now that school is over, and this: every day (!) without leaving a trace of damage and chaos behind them.

At some stage I decided to take the phenomenon of lining up in pairs as a topic for a detailed analysis. By using the toolbox of Michel Foucault together with material from a psychoanalytic background it was possible to explain the dynamics within educational institutional contexts that lead to the implementation of the practice of lining children up. I found that this activity is best understood as a ritualised activity. As such it is essentially linked to the generation, up-keeping, challenging, reforming, hence the negotiation of power relations.

However it is not the only ritualised activity that happens in educational institutions. On a closer look it becomes obvious that in these places an incredible amount of ritualised activities are observable.

For years I tried to bring up these issues in reflection settings with colleagues. This proved to be difficult. The particular problem of reflection on rituals stayed with me also when I settled in Ireland in 2000. Similar to Germany, I found that in Irish schools there were numerous ritualised activities. And similar also to Germany I found that it was difficult to discuss these activities with teachers. This led to the development of a concept for a research project about reflection processes of teachers on rituals in school. This study was carried out between 2010 and 2013 with primary school teachers in Ireland and Germany.

In the course of the research I noticed that there is little coherence in the international debate on rituals in education. Particularly the lack of reciprocal fecundation of contributions from an English and a German background constitutes a significant gap. In the first chapter I provide a comprehensive overview about the instruments that are suggested for ritual analysis of education in these contributions.

Ritual analysis is still a rather marginal approach in the field of education. This is unfortunate. The potential of ritual analysis for engaging with educational practice is huge. In taking conceptual ideas of ritual analysis as a starting point it is possible to focus strongly on issues like order, norms, value systems, beliefs, power structures, all of which are inherently connected to institutional education. In this sense ritual analysis can be seen as a tool for reflection on educational practice.

The study included a comparative element. Teachers from Irish primary schools, German mainstream schools and German free alternative schools took part in it. The free alternative schools offered a field where the social order is based on a radical democracy without formal hierarchies. Here children are not subjected to a set curriculum, they are free to decide what, when, where, and with whom they want to do. A general sketch of the free alternative schools is included in chapter two. In chapter three space will be given to ritual cultures in the different schools.

Chapter four presents a sketch of conceptual ideas on reflection. Processual scale, functional and orientational character are identified as models for a classification of reflection processes. However there are limitations in these models. Therefore in chapter five I suggest to enhance the figures of thought applied to concepts of reflection and systematically take into account the character of reflection as a social act. This approach provides the basis for extensive coverage of reflection processes of teachers on their ritual practices. They are analysed in accordance with the model of reflection as a social act. It will become clear that these reflection processes are best understood as negotiations of legitimacy of defining, articulating and shaping reality.

Particular attention will be given to the idea of critical reflection in chapter six. Here a change in perspective is suggested that leads to asking questions of the actors rather than the act in rituals.

In making the material compiled in this book available I hope to incite further engagement with ritual analysis and critical reflection in education practice.

Chapter 1 School and Ritual

1.1. Introduction

Rituals have been linked to education, and education to rituals merely in passing since the early parts of the 20th century. In 1925 Siegfried Bernfeld's essay *Sisyphus or The limits of Education* refers to education in school as a derivation of rites in tribal societies (Bernfeld 1973, p. 43). Willard W. Waller finds in education complex rituals of personal relationships, on which a moral code is based as well as a set of folkways, mores, and irrational sanctions (Waller 1932, p. 96).

However there is a certain fuzziness surrounding the term ritual. The difficulties of unambiguously defining ritual have been highlighted numerous times (e. g. Bell 1992, Dücker 2007). There is no universal definition of ritual even in the general field of ritual studies. In line with this there are also quite different approaches in the context of debates on rituals in school. Accordingly the spectrum of concrete activities within schools that are considered to be rituals is rather diverse. It ranges from rather minute acts like greeting each other in the morning to rather extensive sequences of acts like graduation ceremonies. In the course of reading this chapter a substantial number of those activities will be mentioned in the relevant context.

I am going to present a substantial overview of contributions made on rituals in school. I will take into account the major publications from an English speaking background since 1966. The debate on rituals that developed in German educational science will also be considered.

An initial step towards a more specific engagement with the topic of rituals in schools was made by Peter Fürstenau in 1962. In a lecture presented in the Institute for Psychoanalysis and psychosomatic Medicine, Frankfurt/M. he spoke about the psychoanalysis of school as an institution. The lecture was subsequently published in 1964. In the context of German educational science his text can be seen as a classic contribution that is still referred to in contemporary literature on rituals in school. However in the English speaking world the text does not feature at all, most likely due to the fact that it has never been translated.

The first major text on rituals in school that appeared in English is the essay of Basil Bernstein/Lionel Elvin/Richard Peters titled *Ritual in Education* which was written in 1966. These two remarks are sufficient to mark a historical starting point for the engagement with ritual in education.

The sections on conceptual thoughts, typologies and aspects of rituals are meant to provide an overview on the theoretical tools that are at hand for an engagement with rituals in schools. However a brief section will be included in the chapter also in which the specific direction will be attended to that discussion on rituals in school took in Germany.

It will become clear soon that there is a great variance prevalent in the debates on rituals (not only) in school. I am not attempting to smooth this picture in a bid to give the various contributions an appearance of coherency that in reality is not there. Nevertheless I will also present the suggestion of Catherine Bell to overcome certain difficulties resulting from the historical appropriation of the topic of ritual in various scientific disciplines. Her proposal to investigate ritualisation instead of ritual leads to questions to be asked not of ritual but of the actors in ritual.

Eventually a section in which the main facets of the problem of reflection on rituals are depicted will conclude this chapter.

1.2. Conceptual Thoughts on Ritual in School

Conceptual thoughts on rituals in school can be found in the English contributions and those from a German background, too.

Bernstein/Elvin/Peters introduce their essay with a description of ritual as generally referring to a relatively rigid pattern of acts (1975, p. 160). It is specific to a situation and constructs a framework of meaning over and beyond the specific situation. They also explicate for rituals a number of functions, characteristics and develop a categorization of rituals. We will come to these aspects soon.

For Franz Wellendorf (1973/1979) rituals are typical scenes in school. They provide a key for understanding the context of meaning in which the individuals in the social system of school find themselves, the interaction patterns and the identity patterns that are on offer in school and the problems arising from the attempt to bring personal historical interpretations of instinctual impulses and affects into the interaction processes in school.

Also with Wellendorf one can see school rituals as *institutionalized patterns of interpretation of social identity* for all participants. Essential for his approach is the assumption that ego identity[1] is not a fixed property. It rather has to be seen as the current identity-balance achieved in a process of identity bargaining (Wellendorf 1979, p. 35, 48).

Identity balance (as a result of identity bargaining) has two dimensions:

- on a horizontal level the problem of integration of diverse social identities assigned to an individual in different social settings, e. g. family, peer group, school;
- on a vertical level the individual biography of an individual with its resulting historical interpretations of instinctual impulses and affects which need to be re-interpreted in new situations.

In the process of identity-bargaining rituals in school present institutionally acceptable forms of common emotions, unified motivation and corresponding action. As such they in fact determine the social identity of the interaction partners.

For the purpose of an ethnographic research project in a Catholic Secondary School in Canada Peter McLaren develops a "weak definition" as his point of departure. For him "ritualisation is a process which involves the incarnation of symbols, symbol clusters, metaphors, and root paradigms through formative bodily gesture." He speaks of rituals as forms of enacted meaning. For social actors rituals allow them to frame, negotiate, and articulate their phenomenological existence as social, cultural, and moral beings (McLaren 1986, p. 48).

1 In his use of the term Wellendorf refers to Erik H. Erikson who states, e. g. "The form of ego identity is more than the sum of the childhood identifications. It is the accrued experience of the ego's ability to integrate these identifications with the vicissitudes of the libido, with the aptitudes developed out of endowment, and with the opportunities offered in social roles. The sense of ego identity (…) is the accrued confidence that the inner sameness and continuity are matched by the sameness and continuity of one's meaning for others" (Erikson 1950, p 228).

Richard Quantz (1999) suggests that ritual may simply be an analytical category that may help to put human experience into a coherent framework. In his sense definitions of ritual are neither right nor wrong, but more or less useful to gain an understanding of the world. Quantz comes up with the definition of ritual as *formalised, symbolic performance*. All three elements in this definition are important. It is their connection that makes an act into a ritual. In his opinion many actions appear only partially ritualistic and he emphasizes that it is more important to recognise the *aspects* of a social act that are formalised, symbolic performances, than come to a strict definition of the act as either ritual or not. One should think of a continuum in which social acts are seen as more or less ritualized.

In Hauke Piper's view rituals are inherently ambiguous. He finds that they are located within fields of tension (1997, p. 220): form vs. content, specificity vs. routine, distance vs. bond, reflection vs. absorption, individual vs. community, emotion vs. rationality. Due to the ambiguity that results from oscillating between the various poles he sees rituals as staged contrariness and he concludes that they are always somehow contradictory staged.

A slightly more technical definition of rituals can be found in Christoph Wulf's essay from 2006. He addresses a number of issues arising from the various debates around the idea of ritual as performative practice. He explains that in his opinion one can only speak of ritual acts if they are mimetic. This includes three conditions all of which are to be met:

- they are movements referring to other movements;
- they can be considered as physical scenes which in addition possess a representative as well as a demonstrative aspect;
- they are not just autonomous and admit of being understood in themselves, but also make reference to other acts or other worlds.

In his definition he explicitly excludes acts of a *non*-physical nature (Wulf 2006, p. 205).

For Michael Göhlich rituals are repeated interaction patterns. In rituals bodily-sensual expressions, stylized gestures and scenic arrangements are the means to constitute boundaries, order and norms of a community and deal with these boundaries, order and norms (Göhlich 2004, p. 22).

Ralf Bohnsack (2004) sees ritual action as a specific form of habitual action. Habitual action (and thus: ritual action) constitutes an elementary form of social action. In his view it can not sufficiently be described with models of instrumental rationality. Its meaning is not primarily found in the idea, the motive or intention, but rather in the empirically observable modus operandi, the execution or production of the action.

In the opinion of Jeanette Boehme (2004), to speak of a ritual in school there has to be a structural potential that establishes a specific leeway for a mediation of meaning and identity for a school (= myth) and also as a blueprint for an imaginary solution for structural crises that are based on inherent contradictions and paradoxes of school practice. Rituals are the arena where imaginary solutions get connected with the school's self-image, meaning, identity. In this sense ritual is seen as an arena for negotiating school myth, and every activity that is not geared towards this process is excluded, hence seen as not-ritual. With her approach Jeanette Boehme attempts to counter what in her eyes constitutes a dilution and trivialization of the term ritual, e. g. its application for interactions in school like the opening of a lesson. While she sees such a situation also connected to an imaginary, mythic level (and having meaning and identity beyond the actual act), what is missing in her understanding here is the leeway for negotiation of the mythic dimension. Consequently for her this is not to be subsumed under the term ritual (Boehme 2004, p. 248).

1.3. Typology and Classifications of Rituals in School

General concepts of ritual serve as a means to distinguish between activities that are either ritual or not. Once a certain set of activities is understood to have the relevant qualities to be seen as ritual it is furthermore possible to look at these activities in a comparative manner. By doing so one arrives at a more distinct classification, or typology.

To develop a typology it is however necessary to define a point of reference, a yardstick that functions as a measuring device for sorting a particular ritual into a certain category or class. Three such yardsticks are present in the literature on rituals in school. They are sorted either by scale, by function, or by ownership. I will attend to them in turns.

When looking at the various typologies and classifications it is necessary to keep in mind that they are analytical categories that start from different points of departure, which consequently leads to developing different descriptive tools. These are however not exclusive of each other. Their separation is more a means of gaining descriptive clarity.

1.3.1. Scale

A first point of reference for classifying rituals in school is their scale in terms of numbers of participants, periodicity, duration of the activity, planning or preparatory efforts. As easy as it is to see the differences in scale of the phenomena that are subsumed under the term ritual in the relevant literature, there is yet a rather peculiar lack of terminology that captures this in clear terms.

For Franz Wellendorf ritual comprises ceremonies, celebrations, special performances, but also everyday school interactions (morning rituals, prayers, lining up). He acknowledges the difference in scale by distinguishing into *rituals* and *everyday rituals*. For the latter he also uses terms like *small rituals* or *ritual partial activity* and he recognises a great number of these in the everyday happenings within school, e. g. lining up after break time, entering of the school-building in a set order according to age, morning rituals like songs, prayers (Wellendorf 1979, p. 89).

The practical approach to including activities as various in scale as a graduation ceremony and a morning prayer is widely repeated in the literature on rituals in school (e. g. McLaren 1986, Henry 1993, Eckstein 1999, Kellermann 2008, Xiao 2008), although there are also examples in which the authors reject the suggestion that small scale everyday activities should be treated as rituals in school (Kapferer 1981, Boehme 2004).

Introducing a nomenclature that addresses the variety in scale Mary Henry speaks of *high rituals*, that is ceremonies, formal events conducted according to a deliberate and correct procedure, in contrast to *low rituals*, that is everyday events, ordinary and practical which have been sanctified (Henry 1993, p. 136).

Another attempt to capture scale differences in a working term is made by Peter McLaren who distinguishes *micro-rituals* from *macro-rituals* (McLaren 1986, p. 79). Micro-rituals for McLaren comprise of the individual lesson in school, while macro-rituals are the sum of all lessons, i. e. the entire school day.

Both classifications (high/low, micro/macro) however did not gain any significance in the subsequent discussion of rituals in school. In the case of replacing *lesson* by *micro-ritual*, and *school day* by *macro-ritual* it is obvious that there may be no need for a new term, the old one is clear enough. In the case of high and low rituals the problem that is inherent in attempts to classify rituals according to scale remains: the scale is at any rate a sliding scale and while the extremes may be simple enough to determine as high or low, when it comes to those activities that are somewhere in the middle, the terms lose their sharpness.

1.3.2. Functions

The second way to approach the problem of typology and classification goes the route via functions of rituals.

The early essay of Bernstein/Elvin/Peters contains such a classification. They distinguish between *consensual* and *differentiating* rituals (1975, p. 160). In their terms consensual rituals are those which function to bind a school community together (examples: assemblies, ceremonies). Differentiating rituals function to mark off different groups within the school community (along: e. g. age; sex; age relations; house).

These thoughts are taken up by Franz Wellendorf who maintains that in every school ritual both aspects are detectable. Their effects indeed rest on the simultaneous presence of both aspects, whereby the accent lies in the display of solidarity at one time and in the display of difference at another time (Wellendorf 1979, p. 73).

Nathalie Gehrke finds it helpful to look at a school class as a type of tribe. In her opinion it makes sense to sort rituals in school according to three primary functions benefiting the group (Gehrke 1979, p. 106). She thus speaks of status rituals (establishing and expressing teacher/pupil status), rituals for soothing conflict (promoting common welfare), and rituals for crisis control (dealing with transitional crisis/rites of passage).

Functional classification is also applied by Peter McLaren. He lists: rituals of revitalization (injecting a renewal of commitment into the motivation and values of participants), rituals of intensification (sub-type of revitalization, aiming at emotional recharge without necessarily enforcing values or goals) and rituals of resistance (McLaren 1986, p. 80).

The dimensions as stated in Nathalie Gehrke's and Peter McLaren's functional categories are also contained in the more encompassing catalogue presented by Christoph Wulf. His classification of rituals includes rites of passage, rituals of inauguration or of assuming office, calendar rituals, intensification rituals, rituals of rebellion, interaction rituals (Wulf 2006, p. 206).[2]

1.3.3. Ownership

The earlier contributions on rituals in school (Bernstein/Elvin/Peters, Fürstenau, Wellendorf, Gehrke) all deal with rituals that are initiated by school officials, mainly teachers. Bernstein/Elvin/Peters in the concrete situation of Britain in the mid-1960's suggest a potential for a switch from the dominance of adult-imposed and regulated rituals to the dominance of rituals generated and regulated by youth. They see a chance for pupils to generate their own consensual and differentiating

2 The classification of rituals is a major problem within ritual studies itself. Catherine Bell comments on this: "The more complete and non-reductive a system attempts to be, (…), the more unwieldy it can be to use." (Bell 1997, p. 94) Christoph Wulf's classification then is quite close to the categories that she presents as a compromise between complete and useful: rites of passage, rites of exchange and communion, calendrical rites, rites of affliction, feasting/fasting/festivals, political rites.

rituals in order to assist in the development of a transitional identity in schools that become de-ritualised. (1975, p. 164) However in their essay they don't address this issue any further.

With Peter McLaren's study a shift in focus took place. He introduced a point of view that also considers activities initiated by students/pupils under the general category of ritual in school. A particular push for such a wider view has been the work done over the last decade by the research group in the Berlin ritual studies. Activities like Go Go-games in the school playground (Wulf et. al. 2010, p. 81), activities during transitional phases from yard to classroom (Wagner-Willi 2005) or helping each other during class instruction (Kellermann 2008) are subsumed under the term ritual.

Further to the dimensions of analysis that categorises these activities along lines of scale or function a new aspect is addressed by the distinction introduced by Ralf Bohnsack which I call the aspect of *ownership*. Bohnsack suggests looking at rituals in relation to their character as being communicative, conjunctive or experimental (Bohnsack 2004). He derives the terms communicative and conjunctive from Karl Mannheim's sociological theory of culture and its knowability (Mannheim 1982, pp 141 ff).

Monika Wagner-Willi explicates this categorization by applying it in her study on transitional phases between lessons and break time (2005, p. 42). With Mannheim she notes that there are two fundamentally different modes of experience or relationships: the conjunctive which is based on immediate understanding and the communicative which is based on reciprocal interpretation.

Conjunctive relationships are based on habitual consent, on understanding each other in the medium of self-evidence. Habitual consent depends on practical knowledge which needs to be acquired through lived praxis. The process of acquisition is mimetic and the knowledge remains mostly pre-reflexive. Transmission of such habitual knowledge takes place mainly in ritual form (Bohnsack 2004, p. 84).

In communicative spaces of experience actors need to mediate (negotiate) their various perspectives. Coming from different conjunctive spaces of experience habitual consent can not be presumed amongst them. Interpretations of social reality differ and on this basis they create their social relationships. Institutions where actors participate in different roles are seen as “communicative collectivity” (Wagner-Willi, p. 43).

Monika Wagner-Willi claims that this difference must not be neglected in studies of ritual action. She follows Ralf Bohnsack in stating that communicative rituals are determined by aspects of exteriority and coercion, are orientated towards codified rules and norms and are highly institutionalized. In line with the conceptual assumption that rituals are forms of habitualised action communicative rituals derive from institutional rules if the rules are internalized and habitualised and thus become rituals.

Conjunctive rituals and ritualisations on the other hand are those ritual forms which take place within conjunctive spaces of experience. They are based on habitual consent, atheoretical and pre-reflexive forms of understanding amongst actors. Conjunctive spaces in school are those that are not under immediate control of institutional rules. This idea is similar to conceptual thoughts of Peter McLaren who presented a model of four states between which students (or pupils, as the case may be) transit numerous times during a school day: home-state, school-state, sanctity-state and streetcorner-state (McLaren 1986, pp. 83 ff). The streetcorner-state resembles the idea of conjunctive space amongst peers quite closely.

The categorization along the lines of communicative/conjunctive as suggested by Ralf Bohnsack can be seen as referring to the ownership of the respective ritual. I borrow the term ownership from Catherine Bell who used it in relation to the historic process in which “social control via coercive strategies demanding personal presence and explicit conflict (…) shift to social control via ownership of the means by which 'reality’ is articulated for cognitive endorsement by all” (Bell 1992, p. 131).

Communicative rituals fit the idea of being means for articulation of reality. In school they are 'owned’ by the official representatives of the institution. Conjunctive rituals can similarly be understood as articulation of reality, yet they are 'owned’ by the conjunctive experiental community (Mannheim 1982, p. 194) that enacts it. It is tempting to equate official representatives with adults (and more specifically with teachers), and experiental community with students, pupils, peer group. Yet such an equation is too simple. Monika Wagner-Willi has shown that in school one can identify "several communicative microrituals"[3] that are initiated and performed by pupils (Wagner-Willi 2005, p. 116 ff). However in terms of ownership these rituals are owned by the children *in identification with their official, institutional role as pupils*.

In theory it is also possible to think of teachers initiating and (co-)owning conjunctive rituals in school. However the practical problems that are connected with a (temporary) shift of positions weigh heavy. Franz Wellendorf has covered the issue of teachers distancing themselves from their official role extensively in a chapter on the ritualized display of social identity and role distance (Wellendorf 1979, pp. 147 – 175).

Here it may suffice to note that while in terms of classification of rituals in school communicative rituals are more likely to be owned by teachers, this is not exclusively the case. However conjunctive rituals in school are most likely initiated and owned by the children. Monika Wagner-Willi observes that in contrast to communicative rituals they are not subject to a formal authority structure (Wagner-Willi 2005, p. 285).

It seems more accurate then to see the factor that decides about potential initiation and ownership of conjunctive rituals in the context in which the actors find themselves. Only where in this context they can define themselves as in opposition to (the demands of) an official authority or where this context is defined as free from an official authority will they be able to initiate and own conjunctive rituals.

In institutional contexts Ralf Bohnsack sees a distinct connection between communicative and conjunctive rituals. He notes that communicative rituals are mediated by conjunctive ritualisations (Bohnsack 2004, p. 88). In addition to the two classes of ritual he also maintains that in circumstances of eroding tradition new and experimental rituals can emerge. Drawing on studies of youth cultures he maintains that particularly young people (adolescents) are likely to develop what he terms experimental rituals in an undirected collective process of seeking in the hope of developing new milieus or elements of style (Bohnsack 2004, p. 81). In terms of rituals in school Monika Wagner-Willi sees these experimental rituals as being likely to appear in

3 The use of the term 'microritual' in her case is not at all related to the suggested classification of Peter McLaren. It is a mere signifier for the scale of the respective activity as to be small, a short (inter-)action in passing.

those spaces and at those times where neither the official institutional order nor the conjunctive peer group culture is in fact valid (Wagner-Willi 2005, p. 288).

The classification as suggested by Ralf Bohnsack allows looking at rituals in school as a dynamic process in which the actors make their respective moves in a dialectical relationship that is essentially structured by the institutional context in which they meet. In this sense it is also compatible with Franz Wellendorf's idea of rituals as factors in a process of identity-bargaining.

1.4. Aspects of Rituals

Not all authors who wrote about rituals in school explicate their concept of ritual to the point where a distinct definition appears. However all contributions on rituals in school state certain elements that in the view of the author are characteristics of rituals. Similarly there is usually expressed an understanding of what function a ritual has. In many cases the actual way rituals are enacted is addressed or the efficiency of rituals is looked at.

It is quite easy to get lost in the multiplicity of statements, in their interdependence and cross-references. What follows in the next sections is a collection of aspects that are construed in the literature as elements of rituals in schools. By grouping various complexes under summarizing headings I intend to address them in a way that is comprehensive and comprehensible at the same time.

I will attend to: communication; actors/audience; structure of rituals; social order, norms, values; dealing with differences; ritual dynamics, ritual effects; conditions for efficiency, outcomes; psychodynamics of rituals in school; ritual style – rituals as indicators. However I am not suggesting that this could lead to a coherent and overarching list of ritual characteristics that would be universally applicable for classification purposes.

The emerging discipline of ritual studies itself can not provide such a coherent collection. Burckhard Dücker points to the fact that in ritual studies an open register of characteristics is used[4] of which for each ritual at least some characteristics are applicable. (Dücker 2012, p. 166) Dücker also notes that "the term 'ritual' (…) depicts a mode of action and a type of acting derived from it, but not a restricted register of acts." With Catherine Bell he points out that in principle every act can be made a ritual when it is formed and organised accordingly. In this sense ritualisation depicts the transition of a routine activity to a ritual act (Dücker 2007, p. 31).

I am going to attend to Catherine Bell's suggestion to investigate ritualisation rather than ritual in detail below (see section 1.6). First I wish to show how the problem of coming to a clear list of characteristics of rituals is mirrored in the literature on rituals in school and how the respective authors emphasise quite a variety of aspects.

1.4.1. Communication

Bernstein/Elvin/Peters refer to the "highly redundant form of communication" within ritual, whereby "the messages (…) contain meanings which are highly condensed. Thus the major meanings in ritual are extra-verbal or indirect; for they are not made verbally explicit." And they conclude that: "Ritual is a form of restricted code" (Bernstein/Elvin/Peters 1975, p 163).

For Franz Wellendorf the scenic-situational aspect of the performance is dominant in rituals. He sees communication in rituals taking analogic

4 Burckhard Dücker lists: intentionality/target orientation; symbolism; framing; narrative structure; repetitiveness; staging; performance; sequentiality/complexity; formality/celebration; publicity; transcending everyday ordinariness; reduction of complexity; continuity; self referential; ritual roles (experts, participants, audience, supportive backstage staff, media audience, excluded others).

form.[5] Following Watzlawick/Beavin/Jackson (1967, p. 65) he refers to the characteristics of analogic communication as:

1. The simple negation is missing, there is no term for 'not'
2. Simple logical basic patterns are missing like ‚if then', ‚either – or'
3. The expression of abstract terms is very difficult or impossible.

One consequence of the absence of the simple form of *not* in analogic communication is that in school rituals it is extremely difficult to express something like: "I do not accept the meaning attributed to this activity." Analogic communication lacks unambiguousness and the absence of clear expressions for dimensions of time: past, present, future opens the route for a double, i. e. conscious *and* unconscious interpretation of social identity, while at the same time this double meaning is not open to verbalization. Thus school rituals offer a great chance for unconscious transference of early-childhood experiences (Wellendorf 1979, p 196, 197).

The importance of bodily performance is highlighted by Peter McLaren. Performative elements "gestures, verbal intonation and rhythmic methods of ritualized expressions" (McLaren 1986, p 104) of the teacher become crucial factors. The strength of ritual's ideological force lies in its erasure of the traces from that which it effects, rituals embody meaning, they are enacted metaphors.

In recourse to the verbal and dramatic expressions as observed in ritual Fulbert Steffensky holds that ritual breaks through the horizon of the pure verbal expression. It says something that can not be said in words (Steffensky 1999, p 101). Rituals are seen to "unfold their effects 'in

5 Roxanne Blanford (2009) gives a brief summary of the concept of analogical and digital communication: "(...) analogical communication loosely refers to that which is represented by likeness. In other words, if someone understands that an action, a symbol, or a movement implies and/or infers a particular thing exactly as intended, it is a successful communication. More precisely, non-verbal communication, in which meaning and intent is represented either without words (pictures, drawings, physical gestures), or by indicating something external, can be categorized as being analogical. That is, some "thing" stands for, and is likened to, something else to which the meaning, or idea, is being referred. On the other hand, digital communication is more exact and identifiable in that this form of communication makes direct reference to the thing by its articulated name. Speaking a language and using easily identifiable and concrete terms and words, as when people are conversing, or reading text, is a digital communication."

scenic participation', not in the reflective appropriation of the values and norms displayed" (Combe 1999, p. 108).

Richard Quantz (1999) finds that bodies of actors play an important role in ritual. Any detail of display gestures, mien, dress or equipment can be symbolic if it is displayed for others to observe, and in this case it is ritually displayed. The way actors perform in ritual bears meaning. He also states that for most people this is far more persuasive than any rational-discursive argument.

Christoph Wulf/Jörg Zirfaß note that rituals are performed physically, they are acted out, displayed. In rituals mimetic processes and symbolic meaning are intertwined in a way that they can only be separated analytically. The figurations, sequences and schemata of rituals are engrained in the bodies of participants, and with them also the symbolic meaning (Wulf/Zirfaß 2004, p. 8).

The symbolic use of activities and equipment in schools is also highlighted by Hauke Piper (Piper 1997, p. 219) and by Ingrid Kellermann, who holds that rituals convey their meaning in performative acts and/or by use of symbols (Kellermann 2008, p. 39). Just like Peter McLaren she also refers to the specific techniques used by teachers and observable in classrooms: pronounced use of voice, prosodic use of language, intonation, pronounced arrangement of bodies (or equipment) in the classroom space. These are triggers for the magic charge (the creation of social magic) that is part of the ritual performance.

1.4.2. Actors - Audience

Rituals are seen to be performed and displayed by actors in front of an audience. Franz Wellendorf states: "In rituals ... the context of individual activities of interacting partners with the entire interaction-system is made visible", and "they show to all participants (actors and spectators) by means of symbolic representation which are the conditions for being or becoming a member of the system: which values to accept, which norms to adhere to, which power structure to adapt to" (1979, 67).

Reference to the presence of spectators is also made by Mary Henry who refers to rituals being performed in front of an audience in a public or collective setting. (Henry 1993; p. 135). Richard Quantz (1999) highlights ritual as an action intended for an audience (even if the audience is oneself). He further explains: "the idca that one might perform for oneself may seem strange, but imagine the nineteenth century English colonialist of literary, if not historical, reality insisting on keeping the ritual of teatime even when all alone in the jungles of India, or the single person who maintains the practice of saying grace before eating a meal even though eating at home all alone."

In the analysis of the phenomenon of children lining up in educational contexts I have taken a close look at the role that the audience plays for rituals in schools. I raised attention to the effects on teachers from the (real or imagined) supervision of supervisors (Hamm 1999, p. 28). This aspect will be mentioned later again in chapter three where I attend to the ambiguous symbolic representation staged by different rituals in the same school.

In the approach that guides the Berlin ritual studies ritual is explicitly understood as performance. While this term is used in different ways (see for a discussion of concepts of performance, performative: Audehm 2004), there is yet a quite basic understanding also, that relates to the components of actors and audience. In this regard a performance always relies on the audience, even where in ritual the actors are always also their own audience (Wulf/Zirfaß 2004, p. 27).

1.4.3. Structure of Rituals

Rituals are depicted as activities that follow a set pattern, a structure that is observable and can be deciphered, be it by the participants or by onlookers. This is contained already in Bernstein/Elvin/Peters' definition of rituals as relatively rigid pattern of acts.

Mary Henry describes rituals in school as having a "grammar (…) a set of formal properties that identify it as such. The structure is like a musical score that repeats itself." There is a special timing for each component in the ritual. There is also generally a precise order in which moves/acts are (to be) performed by participants (Henry 1993, p. 135).

In Richard Quantz' definition of ritual as formalised, symbolic performance the idea of formalisation points to the complex of structure within ritual. There is a correct time, a correct space and a correct way of acting (according to the expectations held by those involved as actors and as spectators) that make an activity a ritual (Quantz 1999). Similarly Hauke Piper (1997) and Alfred Hinz (1999) see rituals as activities that are repeated at the same time, same place in the same manner as prescribed. In line with the idea of repetition and structure of rituals in school Kathrin Audehm (2004) finds reoccurring problems being dealt with in reoccurring patterns.

An interesting route is opened by Peter McLaren who refers to the "segmentation of time into 'units' of 'periods' [which] influenced the students' perception of work such that work became time spent 'doing one thing over and over' until the period was over. Time literally became 'death' – an enemy to avoid" (McLaren 1986, p. 198).

The observation that in schools there are numerous sequences of routine activities and routine arrangements is also made by Thomas Ziehe. He finds that these activities are in fact "smallest rituals" that "incite this peculiar feeling for time … everything seems the same, time seems to come to an agonizing standstill and yet years pass by" (Ziehe 1987, p. 16).

1.4.4. Social Order, Norms, Values

The connection between ritual and social order is a topic for ritual studies from their very beginning. It is also a major area of concern for authors who wrote on rituals in school.

While he concentrates mainly on the role that rituals play for the psychodynamics for teachers and students in school, Peter Fürstenau also sees a connection between the ways the participants in a school context interact and the social order in which the school is set. He finds that where children have to basically fit in with a predefined – and on top of that contradictory – order the only possible consequence for them in expressing their drive for emancipation and autonomy will be that they are identified as creating disciplinary problems (Fürstenau 1969, p 24).

The interpretation of rituals in school context offered by Bernstein/Elvin/Peters heavily draws on the issue of social order. Rituals are seen to "relate the individual (…) to a social order, to heighten respect for that order, to revivify that order within the individual and, in particular, to deepen acceptance of the procedures which are used to maintain continuity, order and boundary and which control ambivalence towards the social order. (…) The rituals also serve to prevent questioning of the values and of the social order which transmits them" (Bernstein/Elvin/Peters 1975, pp. 160, 161).

On the last point Franz Wellendorf (1979, p. 70) sees the prevention of questioning the values or social order as expressed in rituals as a consequence of the specific form of ritual and their structure as rigid patterns of acts.

That there are connections between rituals and social order, norms, values is similarly accepted by more current authors. What however changes is that these connections are interpreted differently. The rather static view of an order that is preliminary to the ritual, hence expressed or imposed through ritual has been shifted to a more dynamic model.

Assessments like Hauke Piper's, who finds that in ritual a pre-defined order is impressed upon the participants (Piper 1997, p. 221) stand alongside statements which put an accent on the generation or establishment of community (von der Groeben 1999, p. 13). Mary Bushnell holds that rituals construct and communicate values (Bushnell, 1997, p. 286).

For Christoph Wulf/Jörg Zirfaß (2004, p. 8) in the ritual performance the social is created. That includes the social order in which power relations are expressed, between classes, generations and the sexes. The ritual performance as a physical experience makes them appear to be natural. Rituals conjure social peace, but the assumed consensus often implies acceptance of power relations.

In this view it is still acknowledged that rituals traditionalise attitudes, world-views, values and norms (Kellermann 2008, p. 40), that they mark boundaries and act as a means of social differentiation (Audehm 2004, p. 56). Yet they are also seen to deal with these boundaries, order and norms (Göhlich 2004, p. 22) which implies that changes are possible, too.

Reference was already made to the concept of communicative and conjunctive (and experimental) rituals as presented by Ralf Bohnsack. For him rituals are crucial in the establishment and maintenance of collectivity (Bohnsack 2004, p. 83), which however is not contrary to the dynamic that is contained in his typology.

In fact rituals are also seen to create, interpret, maintain and change social realities by Prengel/Heinzel (2004, p. 116). The dynamic qualities of ritual feature particularly prominent in the surroundings of the Berlin ritual studies. Christoph Wulf maintains that social relationships are shaped by rituals that oscillate between conflict and integration. Rituals can be invented, e. g. in political battles or inter-generational conflict, to draw demarcation lines between groups (Wulf 2006, p. 207). While Christoph Wulf's comment originates from a rather general consideration of rituals, the idea of inventing rituals is very much part of the quite specific debate on rituals in schools in Germany since the 1990's (see: Pädagogik 1/94; von der Groeben 1999).

1.4.5. Dealing with Differences

In their being linked to social order, norms and values rituals are found to be essentially dealing with differences.

As mentioned earlier Judith Kapferer's approach to rituals does not include the everyday activities (small, low rituals) in school. In her terms the rituals counteract divisive tendencies on various levels of school life. She sees this as a result of the extraordinary character of the ritual which is established as an activity outside of routine and everyday practice. In addressing potential division the ritual functions as an expression of unity (consensual in terms of Bernstein/Elvin/Peters). There is yet no claim made by Judith Kapferer that the ritual would factually abolish division, rather is it a case of the ritual making it appear as if there is no division.

She refers in this context to the internal division within the cultural bourgeoisie, the dominant clientele of private schools in Australia.[6] These divisions may be covered up in school rituals. However they do not disappear but rather prevail behind the façade of false consciousness (Kapferer 1981; p. 270).

The assumption that rituals deal with differences is yet also shared by authors whose view on ritual classification includes the everyday, small, low rituals. The concept of identity-bargaining as put forward by Franz Wellendorf in relation to school rituals already includes an inherent division, be it in vertical (social role expectations vs. biographical identity) or in horizontal (peer identity vs. institutional identity) direction.

Similarly the repeated transition from one interactive state to another (streetcorner-state, student-state etc.) as observed by Peter McLaren includes the topic of dealing with differences.

Monika Wagner-Willi looks at the transition between break time and class. Based on the conceptual typology suggested by Ralf Bohnsack this can be seen as transition between spaces of conjunctive and communicative experience. She finds that in the transition periods differences within the peer group find entry into the classroom, are acted out and dealt with ritually. Her study particularly observes this for gender relationships and differences in relation to maturity at the passage from childhood to adolescence (Wagner-Willi 2005, p. 290).

That rituals deal with differences is also part of the general concept of ritual as presented by Christoph Wulf/Jörg Zirfaß (2004, p. 8) and can be found made explicit by Ingrid Kellermann who connects this idea with the assumption that rituals channel aggression and conflict (Kellermann 2008, p. 40).

It is worthwhile noting that the dimensions that are referred to as above by Judith Kapferer and the ones that Monika Wagner-Willi or Ingrid Kellermann have in mind are a good bit apart of each other, the latter being concerned primarily with the micro-level of everyday activities in

6 "The fraction of the ruling group that controls, dominates, and, in an important sense, owns (partly through consumer patronage, but also through public, professional activity) the means of educational production – the dissemination of knowledge, ideas, opinion, and judgments" (Kapferer 1981, p. 263)

school. Nevertheless it is obviously possible on both levels to come to a conclusion regards rituals that sees them dealing with differences.

1.4.6. Ritual Dynamics, Ritual Effects

For participants in rituals it is assumed that there are certain outcomes as a result of their participation. One line of argument refers to ritual knowledge which is acquired by participants: "primarily a bodily form of knowing as opposed to a cognitive skill." Ritual knowledge is not rationally to be understood, it is based on a felt experience and "it is a type of *mimesis*" (McLaren 1986, p. 204).

The importance of mimesis in and for rituals is highlighted by Christoph Wulf/Jörg Zirfaß. Ritual knowledge is practical knowledge, physical, ludic, historic and cultural. By acquiring ritual knowledge mimetically the individual incorporates an imprint of the social as performed in the ritual. At the next occasion this imprint can be actualized in a new ritual performance. However there is never an exact copy possible of the original. This is the creative potential of mimetic processes (Wulf/Zirfaß 2004, p. 31). The figure underlying this is the concept of constant flow. The ideas of mimesis, creativity, performativity applied to ritual introduce this concept into ritual studies. Seen from the perspective of the individual actor, the mimetic processes allow for individual derivation (Kellermann 2008, p. 40).

From their very start ritual studies in general have always seen a close connection between ritual and emotions. In reference to Emile Durkheim's concept of collective effervescence (Durkheim 1947, p. 214 ff) Randall Collins exemplifies this for the sociology of ritual which he identifies as "a sociology of gatherings – of crowds, assemblies, congregations, audiences. (…) Once the bodies are together, there may take place a process of intensification of shared experience" (Collins 2004, p. 34, 35). He in fact ascribes emotions a central status in the context of interaction rituals. "(…) [R]ituals begin with emotional ingredients (which may be emotions of all sorts); they intensify emotions into the shared excitement that Durkheim called 'collective effervescence'; and they produce other sorts of emotions as outcomes (especially moral solidarity, but also sometimes aggressive emotions such as anger). This puts us in a position to use the flow of emotions across situations as the crucial item in the micro-to-micro linkage that concatenates into macro patterns" (Collins 2004, p. 105).

In the context of literature on rituals in schools the emotional charge that is associated with rituals is taken up by Peter McLaren whose field study took place in a Catholic secondary school. His rituals of revitalization and rituals of intensification both contain the element of emotional recharge for the participants (McLaren 1986, p. 80). For Peter McLaren the emotional aspects of ritual play an important role. He identifies spontaneous communitas as characteristic for an authentic or genuine ritual and finds that in school there is a general lack of it, which also leads to him speaking of the school day as "a bastard version of Van Gennep's rites of passage" (McLaren 1986, p. 98).

Thomas Ziehe notes that ceremonies, staged events fill the gap between the individual (subjective) and the formal (objective), they allow for collective effervescence to be experienced (Ziehe 1987, p. 17). For Ameli Winkler rituals are invented realities which – if they are not regulating or schematising – out of nothing create reliability, confidence, a feeling of togetherness and even consolation. She compares them to a "railing that the (child's) soul can hold on to" (Winkler 1994, p. 67).

These rather positive assessments of the emotional side of rituals are not unanimously shared by Mary Bushnell for whom rituals also have an abusive and deterministic potential which she traces back to the fact that "rituals can coerce through their symbolic qualities – rituals get to our emotions." As holistic experiences involving body, emotion and intellect she finds that rituals are non-trivial. (Bushnell 1997, p. 288).

At any rate from the early psychoanalytic contributions (Fürstenau, Wellendorf) to Ingrid Kellermann's recent study who finds that the magic boundary between 'us' and 'them' establishes a feeling of belonging together (Kellermann 2008, p. 40) it can be seen as commonly accepted that rituals have effects on an emotional level for the participants.

Another effect of rituals is observable for those who do not fit in with the actual demand. "Once a pupil has ritually been affiliated to school, there is no institutionally legitimized motive any more, not to follow the expectations put to him. If he still refuses or protests, he becomes a problem pupil who needs special treatment" (Wellendorf 1979, p. 76).

Peter McLaren in his chapter on "the antistructure of resistance" notes that "resisters challenged the legitimacy of the social pressure which read 'You must do this' or 'You must do that'. Resistances often provoked fulminations from the teachers ..." (McLaren 1986; p.149). And in reaction to this "redressive measures within the social drama involved expelling the occasional offender, trying to find a more 'appropriate' programme for the student in another school, and administering detentions" (McLaren 1986, p. 150).

There are consequences for those who do not participate in rituals as expected. While there may be leeway via mimetic performances, this leeway is not endless. Ritual performances invite to play along – and by doing so accept the expressed meanings, structures, order, power relations. Those who don't play along are excluded and can become a scapegoat, a screen for projection of negativity and violence (Wulf/Zirfaß 2004, p. 9).

School rituals are not isolated activities. They are connected in chains, building on each other.[7] Thus they constitute a process of continuous (re-)interpretation of identity (in the identity-bargaining), which leads to a particular 'school career' for the individual pupil/student (Wellendorf 1979; pp 127 – 142). In this way it is possible to understand rituals as a means of sorting out within a school context, a tool for selection.

Jiamei Xiao suggests a different perspective when looking at the effects of rituals in school. Her investigation aims on discovering the experiences of children in their own terms. She presents the results of a field observation and interviews conducted with children in a UK-primary school. Her main focus lies on "trivial everyday experiences" (Xiao 2008, p. 6) and "repeated procedures and routines in the classroom" (Xiao 2008, p. 11) which she sees to have "the characteristics of routine or ritual" (Xiao 2008, p. 69).

For the concrete ways of children's acting in school she identifies "three styles of response in terms of attitudes and actions: acceptance, resistance and reflection" (Xiao 2008, p. 214). Jiamei Xiao finds that "all three responses are reflected in more or less all the children as different

7 For looking at rituals as connected in chains see also: Randall Collins (2004).

aspects of their experience" (p. 215). She suggests that for the children the two contrary responses of resistance and acceptance are co-existent, even overlapping attitudes. She eventually concludes: "On a closer examination the differentiation between the two opposite attitudes (…) turns out to be difficult, even meaningless (…). Children's resistance is a natural, spontaneous response to the rituals of schooling whereas their acceptance is mostly a superficial response based on practical considerations and the pressure to be passive in the face of the schooling system" (p. 236).

Jiamei Xiao's reference to the co-existence of seemingly contradictory effects of daily routines and everyday rituals in school points to the lack of certainty in predicting which result a particular ritual will bear for a particular participant. This is also acknowledged by Mary Henry who states that there is no guarantee of a particular experience to be made by each or any individual participant (Henry 1993, p. 27).

A specific type of ritual are those concerned with change/s of status for participants. They are seen to formally structure access to formal and informal roles within the system (Wellendorf 1979, p. 67). Mary Henry refers in this context to status elevation as an effect of rituals (Henry 1993, p. 40). Status elevation suggests that the direction is always 'up', but rituals are similarly seen to be involved in bearing opposite results e. g. in the context of examinations (Wellendorf 1979, pp 111 – 113).

After all it is a commonly accepted assumption that rituals can have an effect on social status of participants. Kathrin Audehm notes that "the power of the inauguration is such that it changes the inaugurated person. On the one hand the image which others have of her/him and their behaviour towards her/him changes, on the other hand her/his self-image and her/his behaviour to which s/he feels obliged due to the authority and participation in the institution that is ascribed via the title" (Audehm 2004, p 50).

References to inauguration rites are commonly made in relation to children becoming pupils (e. g. Wellendorf 1979, p. 74; Riegel 1994, p. 24; Kellermann 2006, p. 105). However in school contexts adults can similarly become part of inauguration rituals. Enja Riegel gives an interesting example of such a ritual in a school context that in fact concerns teachers and not pupils. "Always on the last day of the summer holidays the first staff meeting takes place. Teachers have breakfast together, they chat. On the floor in the centre of the room there is a red velvet carpet. On it a mandala is formed, a circle of stones, which symbolizes a source of energy. On bare feet a new colleague steps into the middle of the circle. He is joined by the principal. She presents a stone to him. The teacher is supposed to make a wish for his time in the school. The principal proclaims: Now you are one of us" (die tageszeitung 29. 01. 2003).

Literature on rituals in schools in general does not place great emphasis on investigating the rituals of inauguration or initiation that teachers experience themselves. As an exemption Alfred Schäfer's article should be mentioned (Schäfer 2004) in which he refers to the school inspector's visit at the end of the probation year of newly qualified teachers as a variation of an initiation ritual.

1.4.7. Conditions for Efficiency, Outcomes

In the section on structures of rituals it has been already mentioned that there is a correct time, space and form for each and any ritual. Ritual depends on time and space. A certain behaviour can be completely appropriate in one context, but completely inappropriate in another (Gehrke 1979, p. 106). On this basis it is self-evident that if the correct form is not adhered to, the space and time are chosen wrong in or for a ritual there emerges the risk of the ritual not meeting the expected targets. The outcomes of the ritual thus will be doubtful and may not be achievable at all.

Mary Henry summarises what in her view are the necessary elements for a ritual to work: the participants, the timing, the repetitive structure, the order of events, and the 'magic' of the performance (Henry 1993, p. 136). Similarly Kathrin Audehm for whom ritual interaction is directly influenced by the scenic arrangements, use of space and time, the material and sensual conditions of its staging (Audehm 2004, p. 56), and Ingrid Kellermann who finds that repeated interaction rituals make use of settings, specific movements to establish symbolic and classifying framing, so as to distinguish themselves from other situations (Kellermann 2008, p. 40).

A slightly different slant is prevalent in Richard Quantz' and Peter Magolda's suggestion that the continuing effects of ritual on social life rest not on the separation of ritual (its borders) from the everyday life, but rather on the fact that it is integral to it (Quantz/Magolda 1997, p. 228).

The legitimacy of a ritual is also seen to be an essential factor to its efficiency. Pupil's response to rituals in school is observed to be depending on the school's value system being in line with value systems outside of school (Bernstein/Elvin/Peters 1975, p. 162) and accordingly rituals can lose their efficiency if social developments progress and the rituals are counter to new hegemonic conditions/world-views (Wellendorf 1979, p. 153, 165).

The question of legitimacy is implicit also in the references made to the status of teachers as a deciding influence on the effects of school rituals. Rodney A. Clifton (1979) has explicated the consequences for practice teachers arising out of the 'marginal' situation in which they find themselves. He describes that often the orderly behaviour in a classroom dissolves into chaos when the class teacher leaves the room and the practice teacher is left on her/his own with the class with the students not taking any notice of commands of the practice teacher. The main aspect missing for the practice teacher in this situation is the fact that s/he has no official and institutionally sanctioned authority.

The connection between official role and practical "ability to structure and enforce the protocol of the occasion" is also pointed out by Peter McLaren who sees this ability as "inextricably woven into the status of the teacher as an instrument or arbiter of punishment" (McLaren 1986, p. 101) .

The same thought is mirrored in Ingrid Kellermann's book in an interesting passage on disciplining rituals. She explains what she sees as a difference between the disciplining rituals that are initiated by the teacher and those disciplining rituals that occur amongst the children themselves. For the teacher's intervention she finds that "the social magic of the disciplining ritual unfolds through the collective acceptance of the teacher's authority. (…) [In] disciplining rituals amongst the pupils the acceptance of legitimacy and authority amongst the actors is not established *sui generis* like for a teacher, but rather situational assigned or withdrawn" (p. 216).

Ingrid Kellermann does not comment any further on the quite obvious difference between the activities amongst children and the disciplining activities from the side of the teacher in the examples she provides. The teacher's interventions constitute a break in the flow of the lesson, have an expressive function and are exemplary. This is not the case with the children's activities. They are rather immediate reactions to a situational problem (annoyance) caused by another child.

Ingrid Kellermann herself actually notes that while children use a variety of expressive forms (e. g. physical defence or attack, ignoring each other, verbal insults) in attempts of disciplining each other, the ultimate ratio for them is always the appeal to the teacher for help. The catalogue of potential behaviour listed for the teacher (Kellermann 2008, p. 216) comprises of: fleeting gestures, symbolic body language, specific mimic and gestures, ostentatious verbal and gestural reprehension, intentional focusing gaze, verbal and prosodic variations (depending on the situation: friendly-ironic, friendly-formal, sharp-disapproving, accusing-insistent, explicit-implicit).

It is interesting that the more immediate forms of acting on another are with the children. Their techniques are far more direct, and one might assume therefore also apt to incite a direct reaction or result. However that is obviously not the case. At the end of the day it is the official authority of the teacher that makes the difference.

Regarding outcomes and effects of rituals I have highlighted that rituals have as their first outcome the creation of a particular reality. In taking Erving Goffman's four varieties of behaviour for inmates in total institutions as model (1968, p. 61) I found that life in school "establishes a constant process of cooling-down, the attitude to be: 'Be quiet' - the first task of a citizen, rather avoid trouble, endure, stay calm. As long as silence is guaranteed, the machinery rolls on – serving the interest of the institution, a most comfortable way of perpetual celebration of itself. If everyone functions, everything functions. Every gesture of obedience enhances acceptance in the fibres of the body since it is inseparably connected with it" (Hamm 1999, p. 20).

This line of thought can also be found in general ritual studies. Catherine Bell points to the physical outcome of ritual action. “The moulding of the body within a highly structural environment does not simply express inner states. Rather, it primarily restructures bodies in the very doing of the acts themselves. Hence, required kneeling does not merely *communicate* subordination to the kneeler. For all intents and purposes, kneeling produces a subordinate kneeler in and through the act itself” (Bell 1992, p. 100; see also section 1.6.).

Where the ritual is seen as self-sufficient, its effect being first of all its manifestation, the question of compliance, conformity and belief becomes important. Peter McLaren has devoted a section of his book to this problem. He notes “Regardless of the monotonous repetition, the invariance and the formality of classroom instruction, most students conformed to what was required of them, although this conformity did not, in most instances, entail belief. While student conformity did not necessarily symbolize students’ belief in the values of the school, it did serve as an 'index’ of accepting those values.(…) By simply performing a ritual, the participant subordinates himself to that order. For a performer to reject whatever is encoded in the ritual in which he is performing is a contradiction in terms and therefore impossible” (McLaren 1986, p. 128).

Thus each and any effect of a ritual has as its first condition compliance on the side of the actors. It is a matter then of the trajectory that an investigation into rituals in school takes whether authors find this a sufficient basis. Bernstein/Elvin/Peters remark that where the social basis for a ritual is weak, it can become a social routine (Bernstein/Elvin/Peters 1975, p. 162). This can be read as a proposal that from their point of view compliance is not enough.

Andreas Eckstein remembers how as a child in school in the former GDR he learns to say things that mean nothing. In primary school when a teacher enters class, s/he says: “be on guard,” the pupils answer: “always on guard,” formula like, mechanical like a pendulum. Later in secondary school, the greeting formula changes, the teacher says: “friendship,” the students answer: “friendship.” However the formula is empty, hollow, the students realize quite well that declarations of friendship in school have as little to do with interest, care or attention as the 'be on guard' with concentration, activity and participation. From his time as a teacher in the GDR during the 1980's he recalls: "My simple 'good morning' was as much a surprise to the students of year 9 as their unassertive and inquiry-like 'friendship?' to me. Thoughtlessly I answered: 'That we will find out yet.' – Was that a threat? It did not sound like a promise, but then, there was at least a chance of coming together" (Eckstein 2000, p. 52).

Andreas Eckstein does not discuss his experiences in terms of efficiency of rituals. The question that jumps to mind however is what the effects for participants are in the first example based on what seems to be meaningless, formula-like compliance compared to those in the second example based on a spontaneous break of the ritual routine.

1.4.8. Psychodynamics of Rituals in School

The first article that paid considerable attention to rituals in the context of school came from a psychoanalytic context. Peter Fürstenau interprets rituals as defence mechanisms against drive impulses that are experienced as threatening and thus unacceptable. He develops his thoughts in line with the early argument put forward by Siegfried Bernfeld, one of the pioneers of psychoanalytic pedagogy. In Bernfeld's understanding for the adult teacher in school there is an unconscious revival of their own experiences in childhood, including all drives, emotions and attitudes that were constitutive for the relationships with their own parents. What a teacher "does, what he grants and prohibits, is what his parents did to him. In the pedagogical pair group he appears in the double role of child and educator; (…) Thus he faces two children: the one before him to be educated and the other repressed within him. He really has no choice but to treat the former the same way in which he experienced the latter (…) He repeats the destruction of his own Oedipus complex with the other child as with himself. This is true even if he appears to do the opposite of what his parents did to him" (Bernfeld 1973, p. 107).

For rituals in school Fürstenau states that they separate and isolate from the subject matter that is taught all those libidinous and aggressive elements that are threatening within the hierarchical structure of school

(Fürstenau 1969, p. 18). And yet for Fürstenau rituals and ceremonies are also formations in which the repressed returns in a different and unrecognised form. He states that "practising rituals and ceremonies, the dealing with people in strongly stylized form itself satisfies specific drive related wishes, furthermore it leads to a fixation with these wishes and their way of satisfying and it exerts an appeal on the partners for a similar fixation" (Fürstenau 1969, p. 19).

While school rituals rely on psychic dispositions that originate in earlier socialisation processes (Wellendorf 1979, p. 71), they are also seen to be particularly open to satisfy pedantic type of aggression, in the name of order (Fürstenau 1969, p. 19). A rather pronounced example from Peter McLaren: "One of the most telling moments for me was when a teacher, standing with his legs apart and his hands on his hips, 'guarded' the entrance to the aisle where the pupils genuflected towards the altar as they filed into the pew. In effect, the students were literally kneeling submissively at the feet of the teacher, who wore a look of unmistakable self-satisfaction" (McLaren 1986, p. 152).

Fürstenau's study constituted the basis on which Franz Wellendorf developed his theses about school rituals. Fürstenau's view focuses stronger on the psychic situation of the teacher than Wellendorf who concentrates more on the immanent psychic dynamic that unfolds for teachers and pupils in the school rituals. As mentioned earlier Wellendorf's conceptual approach attends to school rituals on the basis of the notion of identity-bargaining.

He highlights that despite the fact that rituals fulfil their function behind the back of the individuals their effect depends on the subjectivity of the participants, too. "They bring with them their psychic dispositions or in negative terms (…) deformations and pathology (…)" (Wellendorf 1979, p. 145), and these for them are the basis on which they enter into the process of identity bargaining. The individual's instinctual impulses, affects, needs therefore are constantly present in all their aspects, irrespective of their fitting-in with the context of meaning.

Turning towards the specific situation of teachers Wellendorf holds that in their role as pedagogues in solidarity with the pupils teachers are expected to understand and accept the individual problems of pupils. Yet as representatives of institutional order and agents of selection they are expected to put in practice the principle of performance and in this role are bound to ignore the personal (biographical) identity of the pupils. Due to their own economical and social dependency within the school system teachers can not possibly openly act against the demands to uphold the values, rules, norms of school (or change them completely). In this situation developing and expressing role distance can be an attempt for teachers to solve the problem of balancing their own identity in face of conflicting demands (Wellendorf 1979, p. 156).

In the dynamics between teachers and pupils the exercising of role distance by teachers actually shifts the problem of ambivalence away from the teachers and puts it to the pupils. They are requested to accept the dilemma of the teacher in dealing with their own demands and implicitly take the teacher's position as their own. By doing so they are expected to take a good part of the burden of the teacher's shoulders and allow her/him to maintain identity-balance without being accused of double moral standards.

For pupils the discrepancy between official role expectations as represented by teachers and informal solidarity with their peers can be a decisive factor in the decision to express their own role distance, and "(…) keeping in view the informal group relations in the context of scenes in school, it becomes clear that the chance for individual pupils to display role distance and personal identity is at the same time one that is allocated by the group" (Wellendorf 1979, p. 162). Wellendorf therefore draws on the importance of being aware of the audience in a particular school ritual to understand the dynamic of the emergence of role distance. Just as much as distancing from the official role can be a criteria for credibility within the peer group, it can similarly be not useful to show role distance openly where there are diverse audiences (peers, teachers, school administration, parents) present at the same time.

No other author has attended specifically to the psychodynamics of school rituals. However there are a number of observations in the literature that relate quite closely to this area.

Writing from the perspective of a school principal Enja Riegel finds teachers often caught in a dichotomy of emotions, a dichotomy of individual needs vs. administrative demands. The space in between these two poles is often blinded out by teachers. This space however provides the realm for "language of symbolic forms" which could "cultivate" it. Thus in her opinion it is important to speak about rituals as a team time again. She also suggests that rituals "give each individual psychological support" (Riegel 2000, p. 21).

In reference to functions of rituals Hauke Piper states that by providing a pre-defined pattern of routine behaviour rituals in general offer a relief of the pressure to decide what to do in a given (problematic) situation. He claims that the development of routines or ritualized patterns of behaviour is essentially something that individuals do for themselves. School rituals however are not developed in an autonomous process by the participants, i. e. the pupils, but rather they are developed, established and modified by the teacher. "The teacher thus becomes the founder of rituals and supervisor of their correct enactment" (Piper 1997, p. 222). In contrast to this in Hauke Piper's view rituals which effectively have a relieving function are to be developed by the group. He also notes that there is a possibility that within a particular official ritual in school a second layer of unofficial "sub-ritual" may develop in reaction to the official demand. These thoughts are quite close to the typology of communicative, conjunctive, experimental as later suggested by Ralf Bohnsack.

It is also clear from the literature that investigations into psycho-dynamics of ritual will always have to look at the school as an institution with a particular influence on the relationships within it and a narrow view from within one discipline can not suffice (see e. g. McLaren 1986, Hamm 1999, Althans/Göhlich 2004, Kellermann 2008).

Annemarie von der Groeben (2000) seeks for the ontogenetic roots of rituals and finds them with Erik Erikson in recognition, primarily experienced between infant and mother, from which is derived a feeling of "belongingness and of personal distinctiveness" (Erikson 1966, p. 605). Echoing this interpretation of origins of rituals Annemarie Prengel and Friedericke Heinzel suggest the examination of rituals in school as the staging of regard/disregard. They present two rather typical examples of staging of a ritual of disregard from primary school contexts in which the assessment of a child's performance is closely linked to the assessment of the child's character. For German schools they also maintain that such rituals of disregard are widespread in all school types (Prengel/Heinzel 2000, pp. 119 – 121). At the same time they acknowledge that alongside there are innovative school rituals (they also use the term *multiple social inventions*) that address the complex of recognition. Exemplary they refer to the practice of circle time in relation to gender equality.

Ingrid Kellermann provides another indication of the psychodynamic qualities of ritual. In her eyes one characteristic of rituals is that they channel aggression and conflict (Kellermann 2008, p. 40). Apart from this more general statement her entire research project is concerned with the process of identity-bargaining of school beginners in the first couple of weeks of their school career. She gives numerous descriptions of ritual activities (of smaller or bigger scale) in which these school beginners are pupilified, i. e. get accustomed to their new social identity.

1.4.9. Ritual style - Rituals as Indicators

Judith Kapferer's essay from 1981 takes into focus rituals in Australian private schools. In the context of her discussion she also refers to the difference which she recognises between these schools and the state schools in relation to school spirit. The latter in her opinion may in fact contribute to the rise of the cultural bourgeoisie by not providing a basic attachment to academic values, and by the failure to symbolically hold them up for collective inspection and validation in rituals and ceremonies (Kapferer 1981, p. 273).

As we have already seen, rituals are commonly recognised as expressing values, norms and beliefs. The lack of a distinctive school spirit observed by Judith Kapferer for the Australian state schools during the 1970's can be closely linked to these schools not having a school culture in the sense put forward by Mary Henry (1993, p. 39). In her terms a school culture is understood to be "a set of relationships, beliefs, values, and feelings shared by those who make up a school" (Henry 1993, p. 39). Rituals are one of the five interconnected domains in which she analyses school culture; the others are: historical/social context; stories, myths and philosophies; curriculum and evaluation; time/space and social relations (Henry 1993, p. 40).

Each school has its own school culture. For different schools having different underlying paradigms, world views and ideals, even the same ritual can signify different meanings, and she exemplifies this with a comparison of advent celebrations in an Anglican high school and a Waldorf school (Henry 1993, p. 171). In this respect Mary Henry's study expands extensively on an idea that was already part of Peter McLaren's book on schooling as a ritual performance who speaks of a ritual charter that he found in the school of his field study (McLaren 1986, p. 183).

In an outlook at the end of her study Mary Henry is of the opinion that it is not possible to "invent rites or any other part of school culture and artificially impose them to 'make' culture. Rites come out of a larger picture which includes the history of the school, the school population, the parent body, the school's traditions, its philosophical and mythical foundations" (Henry 1993, p. 216). In this regard it is interesting to follow up on the discussions in German educational science (and practically in German schools) where exactly this conscious shaping, influencing of school culture plays a big role (e. g. Riegel 2000, von der Groeben 2000, Hinz 2000).

The concept of ritual knowledge was mentioned already. In the form used by Peter McLaren the term referred to the knowledge of individuals about the rituals in their school environment, a type of ritual mastery (Bell 1992, p. 107). It could similarly be called ritual literacy but this term has been used by Mary Henry in a slightly different fashion. She understands this to be "the rituals of a particular school" rather than a certain ability, knowledge of the school population (Henry 1993, p. 171).

Yet another use of the terminology can be found in the article of Birgit Althans and Michael Göhlich on ritual knowledge and organizational learning. They maintain that schools as organisations have a ritual knowledge – which is rather close to Mary Henry's idea of ritual literacy. Organisational learning in their eyes consists of the inclusion of ritual knowledge from contexts outside of the organization, bringing it together with traditions within the organization and transferring it into a new traditionalised ritual knowledge for the organization. School modifies ritual knowledge for its continuity as an organization with specific function, aims and traditions (Althans/Göhlich 2004, p. 207).

In line with the symbolic and expressive character of rituals as rolled out earlier, rituals then can be looked on as indicators. We have seen already that rituals in this sense are carriers of information about the norms, values, beliefs that are constitutional for the school in which they appear.

I have highlighted the fact that various rituals that are observable within a given school do not necessarily all represent the same values, even if these rituals are understood as 'school rituals' or 'communicative rituals.' I have further put this phenomenon into a stringent relation to the discourse on and within the discipline of pedagogy (Hamm 1999, p. 26). Therefore to understand rituals in this sense is only possible if one takes into account the historical situation in which they appear.

1.5. The German Debate on Rituals

As can be seen in the review of literature on rituals in schools I have taken into account major contributions from an English speaking context, but also from a German background. It may be useful to point out that the reciprocal fecundation between these two contexts is rather limited. While the contributions of Bernstein/Elvin/Peters and Peter McLaren enjoy at least a certain proliferation within Germany, other publications (e. g. Gehrke, Kapferer, Henry, Quantz) are often unknown even in scholarly circles.

Similarly for the German texts in the English speaking world: the early contributions from psychoanalytic background (Fürstenau, Wellendorf) have never been translated. The practice-orientated debate of the late 1980's and 1990's (e. g. Ziehe, Riegel, Steffensky, von der Groeben) and the critical contributions of the late 1990's (e. g. Piper, Hamm) are similarly unavailable in English. It is only in the last couple of years that something like an exchange of thought has started. What in fact happens is that some results of the Berlin ritual studies have been published in English (e. g. Werler/Wulf 2006; Wulf et. al. 2010). However to call this exchange of thought a lively debate would surely be an exaggeration. It is a start though.

For English speaking readers it may be worthwhile thus to at least sketch some major lines of the German debate on rituals in education.

During the 1960's and 1970's in (West-)German educational debates the dominant view was that rituals are a means of conservative and even reactionary control. Peter Fürstenau and Franz Wellendorf provided the main theoretical background for argumentation in this context. A view that identified rituals as elements of authoritarian pedagogy was widely accepted. It is also reproduced by Helmut Fend in his seminal publication "Theorie der Schule" where he refers to ritualisations as a means of coercion (Fend 1980, p. 176).

In the context of an overall conservative roll-back in West-Germany during the mid 1980's a new discussion on rituals in schools was triggered which continued also in re-unified Germany throughout the 1990's. The structuring functions of rituals were highlighted and appreciated in various ways. Practical applications of rituals were discussed as solutions for discipline problems in school (see e. g. Ziehe 1987; Riegel 1994).

The importance of periodicals at the overlap between theory and practice for the transmission of lines of argumentation for teachers should not be underestimated. Antje Langer (2008) has produced a remarkable study about contemporary body practices, body concepts and their discursive mediation in the context of schools in Germany. She shows how argumentative figures are disseminated via periodicals that contribute to the interpretation of rituals as legitimate practices in German schools.

Antje Langer has pointed out that rituals in contemporary German schools can be seen as preventive didactic practices. Their desired effect is a disciplining of bodies. "Descriptions of ritualised practices (…) take up the position of a discipline that is thought of as productive. A negative depiction of the term [discipline] as sanctioning regimentation can not do that." In the periodicals which she surveyed "explicit suggestions for body oriented work with pupils" are made (Langer 2006, p. 272). These suggestions aim at the establishment of silence, quietude and calmness.

Antje Langer puts these contributions in a context of a discourse about a reorientation of pedagogy, away from the *poisonous pedagogy* of the past.[8] Discipline in this context is no longer modelled along lines of punishment. "(...) coercion is not desired. It comes to a peculiar constellation: the teachers should achieve a disciplined situation (…) without disciplining" (Langer 2006, p. 272). The solution for this dilemma is sought in ritual practices. They are suggested as means to achieve a disciplined situation in the classroom while at the same time their disciplining character is not discussed.

Rituals of the past are branded for their repressive character. However, modern day pedagogy is depicted as a long way from its dark history. Critical examinations and ambivalences in argumentations are restricted to general discussions of rituals. "In reports from experiences which can be at the same time read as manuals for possible didactic practices, and in the context of everyday school rituals (…) such a problematisation does not feature" (Langer 2008, p. 177).

In a peculiar way teacher educators and teachers seized the concept of ritual and developed it into a whole body of practical suggestions. There is an underlying premise on which these suggestions build. The overall cliché of children's needs provides a killer-phrase[9] in any discussion. It is pronounced that "children need rituals" (Sattler 2007, p. 28). On this basis there is no legitimate questioning of the idea of ritual as such any more. The general desire in human beings to feel safe is translated into the demand for rituals to provide this safety in the institutional context of school.[10]

---

8 I am using the translation "poisonous pedagogy" here instead of the literal translation of the original term "black pedagogy" (schwarze Pädagogik) as used by Antje Langer. The term "schwarze Pädagogik" was coined by Katharina Rutschky. It refers to restrictive and repressive educational techniques that make use of inflicting of pain (physical and emotional), to the total supervision of children (control of their bodily expressions, rigid codes of behaviour, demanding total submission) and to the taboo of sensual physical contact.

9 Stephen Brookfield suggested the term "premature ultimate" for such a cliché that is used in discussion to end discussion: "To claim to meet the community's needs is to assert one's credentials as a humanistic, concerned adult educator. The phrase, therefore, functions as a "premature ultimate" in that its invocation precludes further debate on the adult educator's professional responsibilities. The air of reverence surrounding the term serves to prevent critical scrutiny of what constitutes community adult education." (Brookfield 1985, p. 232)

10 Examples from school programmes in 2012:
"Children need rituals for orientation and structuring in their everaday life. They need quietude to calm down and to contemplate." (Hainwaldschule-Voerum, Peine);

In teacher education in Germany in 2014 seminars on rituals in school are on offer and the notion of ritual as a basic concept within education informs the teaching of teachers. Student teachers can choose to do assignments on rituals in schools. A plethora of publications appeared over the last twenty years with manuals for rituals in school. The most notorious title is probably Astrid Kaiser's "1000 rituals for primary school" which was reprinted in seven editions since its first publication in the year 2000.

Rituals are thus seen not only as a legitimate practice within educational institutions, they are portrayed as a necessity (because: children need them!), which immunises them against fundamental critique. Accordingly rituals are developed into a didactic means that should be standard part of the repertoire of a good teacher.

The choreography of rituals in German schools in 2014 however differs from the one in the 1960's. Circle time is probably the most prevalent example. According to a study conducted by Friedericke Heinzel in 2001, circle time was practised in 89 % of German primary schools (Prengel/Heinzel 2004, p. 122). I would expect that ten years later this figure is even higher.

A teacher in Germany who introduces circle time in the classroom will necessarily have an understanding of this practice as to be a ritual. If the teacher has been attentive during the lectures in teacher training she or he will make pronounced use of symbols, a sound-bowl or a rain-stick may be used to create an atmosphere of meditative silence, a certain gesture may be required from children who wish to speak, a toy fetish may be passed around from speaker to speaker etc.

And in line with the hegemonic discourse in Germany this ritual will be seen as serving a substantial need of children, providing regularity, reliability, structure, safety – all of which are terms that have a highly positive connotation in contrast to e.g. anxiety, strife, restlessness, etc.

"Children need rituals. Rituals establish orientation, safety, trust and respect." (54. Grundschule, Leipzig);
"Children need rituals. Rituals establish orientation, safety and trust." (Montessorischule Reumontstrasse, Aachen)
Like a mantra these formulas are repeated over and over again.

1.6. Changing Perspectives: Ritualisation as a Strategy

In the literature on rituals in school there is quite frequently a use of terminology that includes notions of ritual, ritualisation, ritual interaction, ritual activities etc. In the next section I wish to show how a conceptual difference can be developed if ritualisation rather than ritual is taken as a starting point. For this purpose I will draw extensively on material that has been published in the general field of ritual studies.

In her book on *Ritual theory – Ritual practice* (1992, if not stated otherwise all references in this section refer to this book) Catherine Bell attempts to present "a framework for reanalysing types of activities usually understood as ritual" (1992, p. 219). She suggests a shift away from attending to ritual and instead presents the concept of ritualisation as an alternative. In doing so she reacts to an impasse that appears within ritual studies. A difficulty for these studies lies in the attempts of finding a definition of ritual acts as distinguished from other social acts while at the same time acknowledging that ritual may be a dimension of all or many forms of social behaviour. As we have seen these difficulties are also mirrored in the debates about rituals in education.

Catherine Bell's suggestion is to attend to social action in general and focus on how and why people privilege some activities vis-à-vis others. Therefore she proposes a framework of ritualisation in which ritualised acts are produced so as to strategically distinguish these acts from other actions. In her understanding ritualisation is a practical way of dealing with specific circumstances, it is situational and strategic. Via ritualisation specific acts are established as more important or powerful than other ways of acting.

The physical body of participants is essential in ritualisation. The participants construct a ritual environment which in turn impresses the ritual schemes upon the bodies. Due to its rootedness in the body ritualisation in Catherine Bell's terms is "a particular 'mute' form of activity" which is "designed to do what it does without bringing what it is doing across the threshold of discourse or systematic thinking" (1992, p. 93). The end of ritualisation is a ritualised body that has internalised schemes for interpreting reality in accord with perceptions and experiences of a hegemonic order. As such ritualisation can be understood also as a means of socialization, which makes it an important feature for any discussion about education, particularly where it is seen as a strategy which is situational applied.

At the same time ritualisation aims at producing a certain reality. We came across this motif already in section 1.4.7. where the example of the subordinate kneeler was mentioned. Ritualisation therefore is also an act of production of social reality anchored in the body by means of the body.

Catherine Bell finds that this process, if it is recognised at all, tends to be misrecognised in that the norms, values impressed are thought of as stemming from sources of power and order beyond the process itself. She speaks of strategic misrecognition because the actors in ritual see themselves as responding to a place, event, force, problem or tradition. What they don't see is that place, event, force, tradition are actively created and redefined by their actions. Ritualisation takes place "in lieu of explicit logical speculation," and "is simultaneously the avoidance of explicit speech and narrative" (1992, p. 111).

According to Catherine Bell to get a full grasp on ritualisation it is also necessary to consider the larger context of ritual traditions and systems in which ritualisation takes place. To understand a particular situation in which ritualisation is enacted is only possible if the historical dimensions of the situation, its connection to certain traditions as well as its spatial, temporal dimensions and the role of ritual specialists are taken into account.

Referring to a neo-Marxist discussion as represented by Georg Lukacs, Fredric Jameson or Pierre Bourdieu she recalls the development of ritual specialists in the process of objectification of human beings and their relationships. With the establishment of institutions a body of specialists appears within these institutions who take on a controlling role not on basis of personal presence and explicit conflict, but rather "via ownership of the means by which 'reality' is articulated for cognitive endorsement by all." At the same time the specific institutional authority is backed up by the development of institutions "which ensure that such specialists do not need constant popular support in order to survive" (1992, p. 131).

This can be applied to the role of a teacher in school whose authority derives not from personal qualities but rather from the position as office holder within an educational institution called school. The school itself is integrated in the 'education system' which is comprised of the entire machinery of the department of education, teacher training colleges, educational science, government agencies like inspectorate, council for curriculum development, school psychological services, professional development providers etc. All these various agencies and institutions shape up to a system of specialists who take on the formulation of reality. As a general tendency the definition or reality that is enacted via strategies of ritualisation by official experts ("ritual experts") primarily supports their own status and works toward retaining their expert authority.

Turning to the idea of social control Catherine Bell suggests to view ritualisation as a process of negotiated appropriation of dominant values. Within the actual practice of ritual activity she finds that what is required is little more than minimal consent, general compliance rather than a consensus based of shared belief system. Taking recourse to motives of Gramsci she talks about the way consent of subordinated classes to dominant values is to be seen as negotiated. Such consent simply rests on the absence of articulated alternatives. And with Bourdieu she understands the consent of subordinated classes as complicity with dominant-class values, however this complicity is "neither passive submission (…) nor free adoption (…) It is fundamentally an act of misrecognition by which the dominated class accepts the legitimacy of the values of the dominant class (…)" (1992, p. 190). And yet, this misrecognition according to Bourdieu is essentially a strategic engagement. Implied in the development of the argument is also that misrecognition as strategic engagement can give way to other forms of strategic engagement where in fact there are articulated alternatives.

A view of ritual as a disguise of the threat of physical violence that legitimises power in Catherine Bell's opinion needs revision. She takes up the approach to power as promoted by Michel Foucault. This approach dismisses the idea that power is a substantive entity, like a thing that can be possessed. Instead of developing a theory of power,

Foucault suggests to analyse power in terms of human relations. Power thus becomes a "matter of techniques and discursive practices that comprise the micropolitics of everyday life" (1992, p. 199). From the numerous refcrences in Foucault's writings to ceremony, liturgy and ritual she derives support for the framework which she develops for understanding ritual activities via the focus on ritualisation. She finds that any moderately socialized person obtains a certain sense of ritual and ritual mastery, and has access to a repertoire of situational forms of ritualisation. This repertoire is the obvious effect of the socialization process that the particular person experienced, "a self-constituting history that is a patchwork of compliance, resistance, misunderstanding, and a redemptive personal appropriation of the hegemonic order" (1992, p. 208). Ritualisation then is seen as "the very production and negotiation of power relationships" (1992, p. 196).

The location of one's own actions and lived practice within the hegemonic order along a vision of personal redemption is what allows for the ability to engage and affect this order. This includes a potential positioning in opposite to the hegemonic order, which is yet dependent on this order. The immediate understanding that an actor has of her/his actions and their connection to the order of things may vary from the understanding of other actors or that of the ritual experts.

Catherine Bell is well aware that the consent of participants in rituals can be based greatly on material needs, without necessarily leading to ideological colonization of the consciousness of the participants. Participation therefore is always negotiated participation. She finds the aspect of negotiation also in the way participants in rituals act. "They do so in ways that open up for them some personal and provisional understanding of how the immediate universe works and how they as individuals fit into it" (1992, p. 208). In this notion of negotiation we can find implicit the idea of mimesis as developed particularly by the Berlin ritual studies (and with it the idea of ritual change), but also the concept of identity-bargaining as put forward by Franz Wellendorf.

Ritualisation "implies and demonstrates a relatively unified corporate body" and yet remains beyond the "threshold of discourse of systematic thinking." In absence of an actual exchange of thought on ritualisation in ritualisation, the impression that participants (and spectators) get is often misled to assume a far bigger consensus than there is in reality. The "need to presume at least an illusion of consensus among participants" also points to the limits of ritualisation. If participants do not care about potential gains or costs from not consenting, and if they are not afforded an "opportunity to appropriate and/or resist in negotiated ways" (1992, p. 211), ritualisation as a strategy will not work. And yet such a situation is only possible on the basis of "either total resistance or asocial self-exclusion" (1992, p. 214).

By taking up Catherine Bells notion of ritualisation the discussion of those phenomena in school that are subsumed under the term ritual can be altered decisively. The idea of ritualisation as a situational strategic intervention in a process of negotiation of power relations brings onto the plane the agency of the participants in rituals; their intentions, wishes, hopes, demands suddenly take centre stage, and with it the strategic misrecognition as well as the question of hegemony, domination and subordination. What is suggested here is a shift in perspective.

Looking at ritual for its symbolic, expressive, performative, normative etc. qualities easily ends up in the impression of ritual being a phenomenon in its own right with an existence that is simply fulfilled by the actors. Such a view in a peculiar way only mirrors the often noted camouflage of values, norms promoted in ritual as being derived from some higher authority.

By looking at those acts that are otherwise seen as ritual through the lenses of ritualisation, and situational strategic intervention in a process of negotiation of power relations, each and all of these acts gain a new quality. They are open to analysis as a series of strategically chosen moves of actors.

The various questions of performance, use of language, movement, space, time etc. become mere questions of techniques. Answering them informs us about the internal logic of a given ritual and as such they are worth being posed, in fact when analysing a particular ritual they are essential to gain an insight into the way how the respective ritual relates to other contemporary activities.

What the perspective of ritualisation opens up instead is a new level of questions. These questions are asked not of 'ritual' but more so of the actors in ritual. What is on the table is the whole complex of questioning their acting as reasonable, grounded or explicable. Also on the table is their acting in its ambiguity within a wider social context and eventually the question of articulated alternatives.

1.7. Rituals and Reflection

The phenomenon of strategic misrecognition as put forward by Catherine Bell implies that there is something to be recognised that is actually not recognised – or else something to be acknowledged that is not acknowledged, at least not at this time in this situation. She states that actors in ritual "do not see how they have created the environment that is impressing itself on them but assume, simply in how things are done, that forces from beyond the immediate situation are shaping the environment and its activities in fundamental ways" (Bell 1997, p. 82).

Strategic misrecognition or blindness of practice are phenomena that must have an influence on reflection, in our case: on teachers' reflection on rituals. Where literature on rituals in school attends to the question of their accessibility for reflection this is usually understood as a problematic area. On the one hand there are suggestions as put forward by Enja Riegel who maintains that to gain self-assurance "it is important to speak as a team about rituals again and again" (Riegel 2000, p. 28). On the other hand there are voices who state that, while rituals are reflexive (i. e. they reflect a value system), they are unquestionable, i. e. not exposed to reflection (Wellendorf 1979, p. 144).

The unquestionable character of rituals is also pointed out by Judith Kapferer who furthermore says that rituals are not questioning either. In her opinion "ideas and actions organized in ritual form receive a certain 'sanctity'" (Kapferer 1981, p. 264). Peter McLaren sees rituals of classroom instruction gaining unquestionable status on the basis of pedagogical practices becoming sanctified (McLaren 1986, p. 127).

In rituals a merely pre-reflexive and affect-loaded basis of moral development is seen to be at work by Arno Combe. He holds that they claim the bodily-material, sensual-active relationship to the world and that they are opposed to the culturally dominant habitus of the rational actor (Combe 2000, p. 111). That rituals are pre-reflexive is a view also shared by Ralf Bohnsack. He concludes that while rituals deal with experiences of differences, they do so not in meta-communicative or reflective manner (Bohnsack 2004, p. 83).

In Hauke Piper's opinion the particular aspect of analogical forms of communication is a hindrance to accessibility of rituals for reflection. Ritual cannot be criticized within the ritual. A negation of the ritual implies that one has to step out of the situation and criticizes it in digital form (Piper 1997, p. 221).

For Nathalie Gehrke ritual is symbolic of the participants' belief in a power beyond human experience (Gehrke 1979, p. 103). Michael Göhlich is more specific in his statement that the cultural and historical background, the underlying power relation and the fact that rituals can actually be changed is covered up by their assumed naturalness. However he also maintains that these all can be uncovered by conscious efforts (Göhlich 2004, p. 22), which would suggest that there is in fact a chance to reflect on rituals.

A distinction is made by Monika Wagner-Willi who claims that communicative rituals are reflexively accessible and explicable while conjunctive rituals are only in parts reflexively accessible or explicable (Wagner-Willi 2005, p. 47).

When the various authors touch on the issue of rituals and reflection they however do not expand in any substantial manner on the idea of reflection as such. Questions regarding the accessibility of rituals for reflection, the dynamics or the effects of such reflection if it then happens, remain largely unexplored. Comments in these areas are often rather common sense, yet they are not substantiated for their actual applicability in the reality of school life. Thus it seems necessary to be far more specific when addressing the issue of rituals and reflection.

I have attended to this problem in the context of a study on the professional reflection processes of primary school teachers on rituals in school. The aim of the study was to find out whether those practices in schools that can be understood as rituals are reflected upon by the teachers, and if so, what the reflection processes are like. Assuming that school environments differ in terms of their ritual cultures and also in terms of their reflective practices the study contained a comparative element. Teachers of three different school types took part: Irish primary schools (IPS), German mainstream schools (GMS), and German free alternative schools (FAS).

Findings from this study suggest that the concepts of reflection that are in use in educational science are inadequate to capture the essentially social character of professional reflection processes of teachers. Instead I am suggesting a framework of reflection as a social act which is best understood as negotiation of legitimacy of defining, articulating and shaping reality. I will come back on this issue in chapter five.

First I will turn to some aspects that came up in the course of the study. The effects of national discourses will be looked at, and the ritual cultures in the three different school types will be described. A brief description of the characteristics of the three school types will provide the necessary background to understand the later passages.

Chapter 2 Educational Environments

2.1. Three Different School Settings

As we have seen earlier there is a connection between rituals and social order, norms, values that has been a constant topic for authors who wrote on rituals in schools. Schools are built on concepts of childhood, adulthood that are paradigmatic for their practice. In schools pedagogic and professional discourses are materialised (and at the same time generated). School practice is always linked to particular aspects of these discourses at a given time/space constellation. Pedagogic discourse is not monolithic, but rather diverse tendencies exist within it. This accounts for a spectrum of diverse concepts on which schools are built and consequently differences in terms of social order, norms, values as enacted in everyday practice.

The research project emerged in an Irish context. Therefore it was an obvious choice to consider Irish schools as a first point of reference. Being involved in primary education myself I decided to concentrate on the primary sector. In an international context the Irish primary schools system is unique in that 90 % of all schools are owned by the Catholic Church, and another 6 % by the Protestant Church. At the same time the state finances the schools and teachers are employed as public servants. The religious patronage of schools is a controversial topic in Irish political debate. An initiative of revising the patronage system was started in 2011 when the Labour Party joined the Government (see: DES 2012). As a consequence of this initiative the push for more multi-denominational schools could gain some significance. One has to wait and see what long term implications this development will have.

Irrespective of their patronage in Ireland all primary schools operate on the basis of the 'rules of national schools' and all schools follow the national curriculum. The school day in all schools is structured according to the allocation of times for the different strands (subjects) as derived from the national curriculum. Attendance in the lessons is compulsory for the children. Children have normally no say in deciding who is going to teach them. This is the case also in multi-denominational schools.

As a counterpoint to the Irish primary schools then it was of particular interest to look at schools that are based on principles of self-regulation. In schools were children "decide individually how, when, what, where and with whom they learn" (IDEN 2005) the pattern of traditional power relations that are characteristic for mainstream schools are supposed to be shifted. It would be only logical to assume that this will have an effect on the rituals/ritualisations that are part of the practice in these schools.

Best known examples of such schools in the English speaking world are probably Summerhill School in England and Sudbury Valley School in Massachusetts. According to the International Democratic Education Network (IDEN) there are over 200 schools that offer an education based on principles of equal participation of children and adults and on the principle of self-regulation. In Ireland no such schools exist. In a European context the country with the biggest number of such schools is Germany. There are 87 schools organised in a national federation (BFAS) at present. These schools refer to themselves sometimes as *free schools* but more often as *free alternative schools*. I will stick to the latter term in my text. These schools offered the requested counterpoint to the Irish primary schools.

However looking at Irish mainstream schools and German free alternative schools as two fields for a comparative study was not yet fully satisfactory. While there are certainly differences in the practice in these two school types that could be clearly traced back to differing pedagogical concepts it was also feasible to assume that there might be differences that are better explained on the basis of cultural differences between Germany and Ireland. Therefore it made sense to also include German mainstream schools in the research. They share with the free alternative schools the national cultural background while at the same time sharing with the Irish schools essential elements of organising their pedagogy: compulsory attendance, set time-tabling, teacher's control over with whom, when, where, how and what the children do.

In an English speaking context the historic roots of free alternative schools and their conceptual orientations is still fairly unknown. Thus it seems appropriate here to include a brief introduction into their history and pedagogy.

2.2. Free Alternative Schools – Foundations, Trajectories

The first free alternative schools in the former Federal Republic of Germany were established in the early part of the 1970's as a result of developments closely connected to the extra-parliamentary opposition during the second half of the 1960's. In September 1967 the first anti-authoritarian kindergarten was founded in Frankfurt. The motivation of the founding members was based on an understanding that pedagogy and politics are not separate of each other, rather that all aspects of life were seen as inherently political as expressed in the catchy formula "the private is political."

Monika Seifert, one of the founders of the group in Frankfurt explained: "Every organisation that counters existing social institutions widens the basis of the anti-authoritarian movement, creates within the old society germ cells of the new one. They are an absolute need for a revolution to ever be possible. In this sense the apparently private interests of parents meet with a social necessity" (Seifert 1969/1977, p. 15).

The educational aims of the group were theoretically influenced by psychoanalysis and critical theory. In Alexander Sutherland Neill's Summerhill school they found an inspiring practical model, although they criticised Neill for a supposed a-political stance (Seifert 1969/1977, p. 15; see also Baader 2008, p. 279 ff.). Alternative models of pre-school education sprouted in many cities in West-Germany in the years after 1968, mainly in close proximity to universities. They were mostly located in temporary accommodation in rented premises, empty shops, warehouses. This led to them being named "kinderladen" (Laden = shop), a term which soon became a trademark name for anti-authoritarian kindergarten. However only few groups found the energy to also attempt the establishment of a school.

Instrumental in this regard was the group in Frankfurt. Initially negotiations with the local school authorities led to the establishment of a model project in 1970 with the first generation of kinderladen-children in a local mainstream primary school. The conceptual elements that guided this model was based on reform-pedagogic ideas, e. g.: cooperation, collectivity and solidarity instead of competition amongst children; abandoning of the traditional practice of regular examination and individual marking of children's performances in written and oral tests; teaching at the speed required by the children's learning; no homework; integration of social aspects (conflict resolution) in the classroom practice. Michael Hartlaub and Renate Stubenrauch retrospectively note on these elements of the model project that in theoretical terms they were an "old hat" already even in mainstream education, however their practical implementation was yet to be realised (Hartlaub/Stubenrauch 1977, p. 52).

The plan to continue the model project after 1972 with a second group could not be realised due to resistance from within the state's school that hosted the first group and due to increasing political pressure on the school authorities. Parents of children from the anti-authoritarian kinderladen consequently went "on strike" and did not send their children to school at all but rather educated them at home. Under German law this was, and still is, illegal and an offence. Parents who home educate their children are threatened with substantial fines and imprisonment. (For an overview on the legal situation of home educators in Germany, see: Reimer 2010).

After another attempt to establish a new model project in cooperation with local school authorities also failed in 1973 eventually the focus was shifted to establishing a free school. From 1974 on this project was realised without approval of the school authorities. It took the Free School Frankfurt twelve years of legal battle before it eventually secured the status of a recognised private school.

A part of the adult group that had been engaged with the model projects in Frankfurt came to Hannover in 1971/72. They followed up the ideas of establishing a model project school in Hannover, too. In contrast to the political resistance that the group in Frankfurt experienced, the group in Hannover found immediate support from the side of the minister for education (Kultusminister) and within a couple of weeks they could secure the status of a recognised school starting their work in 1972. Thus the Glockseeschule in Hannover is commonly regarded as the oldest free alternative school in Germany.

The number of free alternative schools increased only slowly over the first twenty years. In 1992 there were 18 schools organised in the national federation of free alternative schools (BFAS). Manfred Borchert in his overview points to the constant political struggle in which many of these schools found themselves in their attempts to gain legal recognition. The school in Frankfurt was not the only one that operated over years in a legal grey zone constantly under threat of closure through the school authorities depending on political opportunities. Others included the Free School Berlin, Free School Kreuzberg, Free School Bremen, Free School Würzburg, Free School Cologne, Free School Stuttgart, Free School Freiburg, Free School Wuppertal. Some of them were forced to close, others could eventually secure recognition (Borchert 1992, p. 18).

Since then the number of free alternative schools has increased faster and in 2013 there are 87 schools registered as members of the BFAS. The orientation on psychoanalysis and critical theory as prevalent in the early models of free alternative schools has subsequently been supplemented by a variety of approaches. In 2013 the foundational philosophies of the schools organised in the BFAS includes diverse ideas. School concepts are influenced by e. g.: Maria Montessori,[11] Elise and Celestine Freinet, Rebbeca and Mauricio Wild, A. S. Neill, or the Sudbury Valley Schools.

2.3. Principles of Free Alternative Schools

The common ground on which these schools define themselves are the eight theses of their educational principles (Borchert 1992, p. 15; BFAS 2014):

1. The present and future problems of society (environmental problems, wars, poverty, etc.) can only be solved democratically by individuals who are able to live according to the principles of personal responsibility and democracy. Alternative schools seek to offer children, teachers and parents the opportunity to practice self-regulation and democracy again and again in everyday life. This is the most important political dimension of alternative schools.

11 But only a minority of the more than 400 German Montessori-Schools are organised in the BFAS (see: http://www.montessori-deutschland.de/einrichtungen.html).

2. Alternative schools are schools in which childhood is understood as an equally respected phase of life with the rights of self-determination, happiness and contentment, rather than simply a training period for adulthood.

3. Alternative schools create a space in which children can satisfy their own needs, such as the needs for freedom of movement, spontaneous self-expression, independent time management and intimate friendships.

4. Alternative schools renounce the use of coercion for disciplining children. Rules and restrictions are created through group processes of conflict resolution, addressing both conflicts between children and conflicts between adults and children. These rules, however, can be changed by the group at any time.

5. Educational subject matter is discovered naturally through the child's own experiences and determined in cooperation with the teachers. The selection of subject matter is a continuous process that involves the experiential background of children and teachers. The complexity of learning is taken into account through varied and flexible forms of learning that involve play as well as the everyday life and social environment of the school.

6. Alternative schools do more than simply impart knowledge to their pupils. They support emancipatory learning processes that open new and unusual paths of insight for everyone involved. In this way, such schools can help to lay the groundwork for the solution of present and future problems of society.

7. Alternative schools are self-governed. The design of the self-government is a meaningful experience in democratic collaboration for parents, teachers and pupils.

8. Alternative schools are places in which every individual's attitudes and opinions can be recognised as open and changeable. In this way, they offer the chance to experience adventure and learn about life.

As a declaration of intent these theses are to be filled by concrete practice in each school according to local understanding and interpretation. At the same time they present a type of yardstick against which the practice of a given school can be measured.

A rather good summary of practical implications of the conceptual framework of the free alternative schools can be found in Gerold Scholz's study about children learning from children (Scholz 1996). In free alternative schools children are not grouped in classes of one and the same age. If formal groups are built at all they usually span over an age period of a couple of years. On a surface level this mirrors the multi-grade classes in small (often rural) Irish primary schools.

For children in free alternative schools Scholz notes "the organising space is not the classroom but rather the entire school" (Scholz 1996, p. 82). This means that children in free alternative schools are not restricted to activities in one room only. They are normally free to move to any room and to any activity as they wish. This leads to an enhanced mingling of children of different age groups and sexes in all sorts of activities.

Children in free alternative schools have by far more time at their disposal where they can determine what they wish to do, what meaning to give to the activity, when to start and when to finish it. As a programmatic element this constitutes as much a freedom as a requirement for the children. "From the beginning the individual child enjoys a great space for making decisions and it is expected from the child that she or he will make these decisions in relation to her or his learning processes" (Scholz 1996, p. 82).

Free alternative schools are depicted as working on the principle of mathetic instead of didactic. Mathetic is the science of learning as opposed to didactic, the science of teaching. The concept of mathetic has its roots in Johann Amos Comenius' work. It was made popular again by Harmut van Hentig. In his expert testimony in the court deliberations on the Free School Frankfurt he described the practice of the school as "not having a didactic, but rather a mathetic" (von Hentig in: Hartlaub 2004, p. 21).

The idea of a set curriculum, seemingly timeless and fixed is simply absent in free alternative schools. For the structuring of learning processes this leads to a different definition of the role of the children. While in mainstream schools the "concrete children with their knowledge, mentalities and interests are seen to modify the lessons (instruction), in free schools they take part from the very beginning in the planning of the activities as to what and how it will happen" (Scholz 1996, p. 83).

The practice in free alternative schools is based on a model of intergenerational relationships that is kept open by the old generation. It is understood as experiment, that is: subject to negotiation between adults and children. Reciprocal demands, expectations, requests are brought into negotiations continuously. There is a constant debate going on, who has the right to define a situation in a certain way, and which definition is the valid one at any given time. Scholz thus creates the notion of *schools of negotiation* for the free alternative schools.

In furtherance to Gerold Scholz it would be worth following the idea of change in mainstream schools, too. Considering the contributions on rituals in schools as put forward by the Berlin ritual studies it would make sense to speak of practice in mainstream schools as similarly in constant change. However such change would have to be seen as in a relationship of constant tension with the overarching curriculum. Actors, children and teachers alike, in mainstream schools thus could be seen as in a position of constantly negotiating their practice against the principles of the curriculum.

Taking Catherine Bell's ideas about ritualisations as situational strategic interventions in negotiations of power relations one has to extend the idea of negotiation. In this sense free alternative schools can not claim to have a monopoly on negotiations. It would rather follow that negotiations about the way "reality is articulated for the cognitive endorsement of all" (Bell 1992, p. 131) are an ongoing process in all schools.

What however differs is the way negotiations take place and the position from which the partners in negotiations intervene, particularly where negotiations between adults and children are concerned. Put in simple terms one may say that the notion of "schools of negotiation" suggests that in free alternative schools these negotiations are taken seriously by all involved and all involved are taken seriously in the negotiations – irrespective of age.

According to Gerold Scholz in free alternative schools the limits of negotiation of children's interests are themselves negotiable. In this absolute manner the statement seems problematic. At the end of the day, they are also schools with certain outside obligations. Gerold Scholz himself acknowledges this when he states: “The free school is first of all another institution with an obligation to attend” (Scholz 1996, p. 82). The fact that adults are necessarily present in the school is also not up for negotiation. This is a simple requirement laid on the institution from outside. However anything within the institution is potentially up for negotiation. Children thus also develop a consciousness of themselves as a status group with extensive rights in the school. This in turn leads to establishing and traditionalisation of a set of norms, values amongst children that are not under adult control. These norms, values build the moral-normative frame for new children starting in a free alternative school.

What Gerold Scholz says about the children establishing themselves in negotiations as a status group and accordingly establishing a moral-normative frame for newcomers (that is: children's culture) is certainly correct – but is is not exclusive to free alternative schools. The difference to mainstream schools is not that there is a moral-normative framework amongst the children. It is in the relationship between the moral-normative framework of children and the moral-normative framework of adults. Gerold Scholz captures this in his remarks that children in the free alternative schools necessarily need to consider the functionality of their children's culture “against a horizon without adults. They are individually responsible for the functioning of their living together because the adults will mostly not interfere in conflicts amongst children” (Scholz 1996, pp. 85/86). Characteristic for free alternative schools is that the children's culture is not normally a subculture in the interstices of the institution. It is in itself openly negotiable, just as much as the moral-normative framework of adults is negotiable, too.

The apparent freedom in free alternative schools can however be quite puzzling for children who are not used to it. The older a new entrant in a free alternative school is and the longer she or he was exposed to mainstream education with it's far narrower scope of negotiability the more likely such a newcomer will have, and potentially also create, problems within the school. This phenomenon is known since the early days of free schools. A. S. Neill reports about repeated experiences of children coming to Summerhill school with a repertoire of experiences from home and other schools that makes it difficult for them to cope with the balance of freedom and responsibility towards the school community (Neill 1982, p. 52).

The concrete practice of free alternative schools should not be understood as if it would be the same in each of these schools. Differences are found amongst them e. g. in the ways how days, weeks are structured, how children enter and leave activities, what solutions are found for conflicts. Michael Maas (1995) raises the point that in the course of their practice free alternative schools came to a position that reconciles mathetic and didactic. He points to examples of free alternative schools in which after a number of years of complete freedom of choice of activities for children a more formal approach with time-tabled activities and prepared lessons was introduced.

In this context it is also necessary to see that each of the free alternative schools is established at a particular historical time and space. Therefore the overall discourse on education plays a role in the concrete formulation of school concepts (and visions of the founding group). Over the 40 years of their history there have been a variety of specific approaches influential in different schools. The umbrella of BFAS and the eight theses as quoted above obviously cover a diverse enough landscape of educational concepts. This can be seen in the relevant references made by the schools in their concept papers (mission statements). The most recent development in Germany sees an increased interest in schools modelled along the Sudbury Valley school where there is no formal element of lesson structuring at all.

Literature about free alternative schools most often hinges on the pedagogical concepts, the absence of a formal curriculum, the idea of self-regulation, the idea of freedom of children to decide what, when, where and with whom they wish to do. This is more than understandable because it is exactly what the free alternative schools put out as their main focus. However in descriptions of life in free schools there is always already included the assumption, rarely outspoken though, that this life is first and foremost established and guaranteed in its permanence on institutional level by adults.

To run a free alternative school it needs an organisational framework. Apart of the formal aspects stemming from legal requirements which are clearly to be fulfilled by adults the day to day running of the school is also guaranteed by adults. Teachers are substantial part of the free alternative schools. However the role of teachers in free alternative schools differs from that in mainstream schools. In fact in many free alternative schools the actual term teacher is not used, but rather consciously replaced by terms like *Lernbegleiter* (literal: learning-companion, connoting a mentoring relationship), *Teamer* (connoting the membership of the adult as part of the pedagogical team), *pedagogue* or *Bezugsperson* (literal: Relation-Person). The squabble with the terminology indicates a substantial difficulty inherent in the free alternative schools. Their attempt to transcend the dimensions of traditional schooling leads to a redefinition of roles also for the adults.

The demands on teachers in free alternative schools are different to those in mainstream schools. “Not always do I find the calmness to face these demands. With my school my habits have also changed. Eventually I am the same person during working hours as I am at home: teacher, mentor, educator, coach, housewife, cleaner, carrier of furniture, and I am a likeable, stern, just, unjust, reliable, insecure, interesting, boring, elegant, scruffy, pleasant, grumpy, old, and not old WOMEN” (Stubenrauch 1992, p. 38). Or, in the words of Christine Pietsch, teacher in the Free School Mauerpark, Berlin: “What is nice in this school is that one is not restricted to the traditional role of teacher of German, mathematics or English, but rather one's personal passions as part of one's one person are brought in also. Here one can be 'human' and act authentic together with children, colleagues and parents (...)” (Freies Lernen in Berlin e.V. 2011, p. 85).

What is depicted here can be generalised as the demand for the teacher to be ready to enter into a relationship with children (and other adults) that allows for more intense engagement than would be normal for mainstream schools. This includes also an understanding of the teacher as a learner her/himself. Yet this learning differs from a continuous professional development that aims on perfecting teaching skills. “Real conflicts include libidinal and aggressive body contacts as much as aggressive behaviour that runs counter to the traditional rules of school learning. Teachers are not normally prepared for these. (…) Problems in school, at home and between home and school are similarly understood as a field of learning as are grammar or fractions. Learning is not the learning of children only. It is similarly the learning of teachers and parents, to deal with the questions that self-regulated learning of children in the school community brings up" (Konzept Freie Schule Frankfurt, in: Seifert/Nagel 1977, pp. 112/113).

The everyday demands on teachers in free alternative schools can be quite high. The intensity of relationships can be overwhelming. Adding to this there is the position on the fringes of the regular system that accounts for a certain pressure to actually show that what is done in free alternative schools is as good or even better than what is done in state's schools. Franz Wellendorf remembers from his time as supervisor with the Glockseeschule in Hannover: "And of course they wanted to do everything especially well, better than the state. And they were very, very committed. They sat in the school for hours and hours and worked, prepared and planned and so on. And for some teachers that was simply too much. (...) Time again there were teachers who got sick and could not work any more, could not work well, were absent, came back, and so on. It was an enormous internal and external demand" (Wellendorf 2011).

Free alternative schools are inherently indebted to the idea of radical democracy. This may have become clear already in the brief on their historical roots. It also resounds in the description of their culture of negotiation as mentioned by Gerold Scholz. The idea of radical democracy as overarching principle also leads to the absence of formal hierarchies amongst adults in most of the free alternative schools. There is no principal, no ranking of pedagogical staff despite the fact that they may come with different qualifications into the job.

Last, but not least, the free alternative schools in Germany clearly draw a demarcation line to mainstream schools in that there are no tests, marks, certificates issued by teachers to assess the children. This does not mean that there is no feedback given to children about their learning efforts. These however are not set against the other children, they are not in form of ranking, marking schemes etc. but rather on a purely individual basis.

Herbert Nagel has rightly pointed out that assessment in schools is a second-order problem. In his opinion the first problem is the equation and definition of "school knowledge" as "generally valid knowledge" and the exclusion of knowledge that is alien to the curriculum from entering legitimately into classroom activities in mainstream schools (Nagel 1977, p. 122). Nevertheless the point that there are no exams, tests, marking schemes, certificates sets free alternative schools off from mainstream schools. As a counterpoint this is particularly important in the context of the German school system.

2.4. German and Irish Mainstream Schools

"In international comparison the German school system is highly selective. (…) The first selective measure is already implemented before children start school: enrolment of a child can be deferred for a year, if the child's overall development seems insufficient. Children in school can be made to repeat a class if their school performance is weak. Children whose learning abilities are too far away from the norm can be excluded completely from mainstream schooling. At the age of 10 – 12 years (…) an obligatory selection takes place into school types that are supposed to represent the abilities of the children" (Bellenberg/Hovestedt/Klemm 2004, p. 4).

I am highlighting the selective features of the German school system here because they play a particular role in the motivation of parents to send their children to free alternative schools, and of teachers to get involved in free alternative schools. The discussion of the selective character of the school system is a constant topic in Germany. Depending on the type of school that a person attended within the three-tier secondary school system chances on the labour market as adults vary greatly. Only graduates of the Gymnasium are able to go on studying and consequently get better paid jobs. In theory changing from one to another school type in secondary school is possible, in practice the downwards mobility is much higher than the upwards mobility (see e.g. SZ 2012).

Children in primary schools are subject to a constant assessment of their school performances. For this purpose written tests are carried out on a regular basis. In the state of Hessen for example the school law requires that in 3rd class in German and mathematics up to six tests and up to three 'learning-controls' are to be carried out. In Berlin a child in

5th class has to write 3 tests every year in German, mathematics, a modern language, science.

Normally these tests are marked in accordance with a scheme of six grades ranging from 1 (the best) to 6 (the worst). Two certificates are issued to children during each school year, one after half the school year is over, the second one at the end of the school year. The written tests count for half the marks in a given subject, the second half is made up of continuous assessment of oral contributions during class. Depending on the results in the end-of-year certificate a child can be made to repeat a year. Besides subject specific performance there is also an assessment of the child's "behaviour in work" and "social behaviour." These are subject to the assessment of the teacher.

There are tendencies within the various states of Germany to reform the marking schemes and replace marks with written reports in which a more general feedback on the child's performance in school, developments in the child's learning, interests or social is provided. In Hessen the certificate at the end of year one is made out as a written report on "the level of performance in the subjects/strands, and also on the development of learning, the behaviour at work and learning, on particular abilities and weaknesses, on social behaviour, on the desire to learn and the cooperation" of children (HKWM 2011, § 14.2). In Berlin for the first two years a written report is issued. There is also the option provided by Berlin school law that the parents assembly of a given class in a school decides that written reports are to be issued instead of marked certificates during the 3rd and 4th year of primary school. This is not an individual right of a family (parent) however. It needs the majority of the parents of the class to agree to it.

It would be a massive piece of work in itself to attempt to give a comprehensive overview of the various details of the marking schemes in all 16 German states and the dynamics of the debates surrounding this topic in the context of school reform. What I wish to point out here is simply that mainstream schooling in Germany is heavily dominated by an ideology of abstract performance. It is this *Leistungsprinzip*, the principle of performance, on which the school assessments are constructed. In concrete terms that means that there is constant pressure on children in school from day one to perform. They are aware (and where they are not, they are made aware very fast by the procedures in school) that they are constantly assessed and judged against each other by the teacher. (For a brief summary on assessment in German primary schools see also: INTO 2010, p. 49)

Despite efforts in Ireland to increase the value placed on assessment and to standardize the practice within and across schools (see e.g. INTO 2010) it is still a fair comment to say that the focus on assessment in Irish primary schools is most definitely not as strong as in their German mainstream counterparts.

Two more differences between the Irish and the German mainstream primary schools shall be mentioned here. The first is the fact that there are still a larger number of small (mostly rural) schools in Ireland in which there are less than 50 children enrolled. 19.5 % of all primary schools (618 out of 3165) fall into this category (DES 2012, p. 31). As a comparison, in 2009/2010 only 72 of 1155 school (6.23 %) in Hessen had less than 52 children enrolled (Hessischer Rechnungshof 2012, p. 258).

The second and most obvious difference concerns the patronage system. The system of denominational patronage of schools in Ireland has been mentioned already. Just recently the advisory group of the Forum on Patronage and Pluralism in the Primary Sector has highlighted the fact again that such a system is “unique among developed countries” and that “there is now a mis-match between the inherited pattern of denominational school patronage and the rights of citizens in the much more culturally and religiously diverse contemporary Irish society” (DES 2012, p. 1). In spite of its apparent mis-match however the system still prevails.

Primary schools in Germany are in general under state's control. The ultimate authority lies with the governments of the 16 states. In Hessen school authority is invested in agencies on a level of the Landkreise (comparable to county level in Ireland). These agencies decide on appointments of principals, they oversee the schools and they are the superior authority in all questions relating to the actual running of the school. (Hessisches Schulgesetz §§ 89, 93) There is no involvement of church authorities in the running of state's primary schools in Germany. There is a small number of private primary schools that are run by the protestant (0.68 %, see: EKD 2008) or the catholic church (0.5 %, see:

www.katholische-schulen.de). The legal status of these schools equals the one of the free alternative schools.

As for shared features between Irish and German mainstream primary schools the legal framework on which they are built establishes a strict hierarchical order amongst the adults, that is principal, teachers, support staff within the school. This distinguishes them from the radical democratic model as mainly followed in the free alternative schools.

In both mainstream systems the guiding idea for the classroom practice is the delivery of a curriculum with a set time allocated to a range of subjects/strands to a class of children of the same age. In both systems it is the teacher who decides how time and space are structured, which activities are allowed at a given time, which are excluded.

In the words of Sheila Drudy and Kathleen Lynch: "The teacher has power and authority over many aspects of pupils' lives. Knowledge, behaviour, speech, and clothing – all come within the sphere of her or his control" (Drudy/Lynch 1993, p. 102). One should add to this list also the teacher's control over physical movement of children. In psychoanalytic terms this idea has been expressed by Franz Wellendorf in a German context. "The 'artificial special milieu' of school (…) has a few characteristics that allow for controlling the interpretation and the expression of instinctual impulses in the scenic arrangement. For the pupils there are created 'uniform conditions for satisfying their drives and interests' so that they are as close as possible under the teachers control" (Wellendorf 1979, p. 202).

Looking at the school situation in "terms of … [teachers'] ... control over pupils brings power to the centre of analysis" (Drudy/Lynch 1993, p. 102). Whereby it should also be understood that a view of relationships in terms of power residing on one side only is too narrow and does not correspond with the practice in schools either. With Denscombe (1985, 129 – 135), Drudy/Lynch note on this quite correctly that "while these aspects of teacher authority are legitimated by the school and by society, the establishment of the teacher's authority does not come about automatically but must be established through the use of classroom management skills, and also through processes such as negotiation" (Drudy/Lynch 1993, 102).

Which brings us back to the motif of negotiation and consequently raises the question about the character of this negotiation. In turn that opens the route into the realm of ritualisation as situational strategic intervention in negotiations of power relations.

In total what makes the free alternative schools a most suitable setting for a comparison with mainstream schools is their abandoning of the didactic principle and the idea of a set curriculum, their conceptual approach to the relationships in the daily practice, their indebtedness to the concept of self-regulation, their conceptual overcoming of the division of learning and living, and their rootedness in ideas of radical democracy.[12]

12 I am far from suggesting that all schools that are organised in the BFAS live up to the same standards in relation to these various elements in their practice. Within the free alternative schools there has always been debates about the correct interpretation of the principles on which they are built. This is an ongoing process and with each new school established there is a new contribution made in the overall debate. For a discussion of the dilution of principles and the tendency to clean out the critical attitude see also Münte-Goussar (2001, pp. 25 – 31).

Chapter 3 Rituals in Schools

3.1. Introduction

In the course of the research project interviews were conducted with teachers of all three school types. One part of these interviews focussed on the reflection processes in which the teachers engaged. Another part addressed the conceptual idea of ritual which the teachers had. Furthermore as the reflection processes were always about rituals in school the teachers inevitably spoke about their ritual practice also in other parts of the interview.

A brief methodological remark before moving on to the actual content of the interviews: Steinar Kvale has highlighted that the amount of interviews used in common interview studies is usually around 15 (plus/minus 10). He suggests that this number may be due to "a combination of the time and resources available for the investigation and a law of diminishing returns." He also states that "a general impression from current interview studies is that many would have profited from having fewer interviews in the study, and by taking more time to prepare the interviews and to analyse them. Perhaps as a defensive overreaction, some qualitative interview studies appear to be designed on a quantitative presupposition – the more interviews, the more scientific" (Kvale 2011, p. 44).

In my own project it was the case that in the series of interviews with Irish teachers there was in fact a stage of diminishing return reached already after six interviews. Themes developed in the interviews repeated each other. I decided to yet include another three interviews in the study simply because I did not trust the low number of references. Nevertheless in the themes that came to the fore in the three extra interviews no new dimensions were developed either.

In the case of the German mainstream schools and the free alternative schools slightly more differentiated responses were generated. However after ten interviews a point was reached here, too, where the themes repeated each other. A specific aspect came into play in relation to the free alternative schools in form of interviews held with different teachers of the same school. In total five such interviews were held (referring to two schools). These interviews proved to be a valuable source of information in relation to the reliability of the interviews. Reporting about their experiences from different angles the teachers of the same schools nevertheless developed similar themes which provided a reassurance for me that the actual data collected could be seen as a trustworthy source.

I am going to attend to

- effects of national discourses on the way teachers talk about their ritual practice/s in school;

- the ritual cultures in the different school types.

3.2. Rituals and Routines – Effects of National Discourses

There is a clear distinction in relation to the way teachers speak about the ritual practices in school. The dividing line runs along the national backgrounds. Teachers in Germany share a common understanding that the term ritual is applicable in discussions on school life. They quite readily speak of rituals as being part of their practice and of school life in general. This is not the case with teachers in Ireland. They don't normally use the term ritual when talking about activities in school.

Frigga Haug has made the point that "language is not simply a tool that we may use according to our liking. Rather, in the existing language, politics will speak through us and regulate our construction of meaning. Thus culturally a number of ready meanings lie around, so to speak; they push themselves on us (...) This happens when we less reflectively and more naively use language" (Haug 1999, p. 11).

Talking about school practice in terms of ritual implies thinking about school practice in terms of rituals. To think about school practice in terms of ritual implies a conceptual idea of what ritual is, does, should be, could be, etc., in short: a theory of ritual.

Morwenna Griffiths and Sarah Tann have suggested that what is often observed as a divide between theory and practice in fact is a false divide. Instead they hold that "what we still tend to label as 'theory' and 'practice' are more accurately seen as 'public' and 'personal' theories" (Griffiths/Tann 1992, p. 71).

For the public theories on ritual in education the overview presented in chapter one gives a fairly comprehensive picture of what is available at this stage of history. For the personal theories of teachers on ritual in education then it is possible to say that each individual teacher has a theory of ritual and as such this is a personal theory. These personal theories are however not randomly formed. They are rather informed by the discourses that are prevalent in the field. The debates, discussions, practical implementations, conceptual descriptions, disseminated literature regarding rituals in education are the basis on which such personal theories are built. In this sense personal theories are not personal only. They are as much social in origin and application as they are personal in appropriation and adaptation.

The German debate on rituals in education as mentioned earlier is mirrored strongly in the conceptual definitions that the German teachers in the interview series had of them. We find a number of motifs in the teachers responses. The first and universal feature that all teachers associate with rituals is the idea of regularity – be it as part of a fixed schedule (time-table) or be it as a response to some particular occurrence.

Then there is the view that rituals provide structure, reliability, safety.

"Aahm, well, it is that it gives the children structure, it gives them a reliable frame. It comes again and again, every week, and the children know that.

(...) We have quite a lot of children in our school who do not know such rituals and something reliable from home, and who are difficult in terms of their behaviour, too, and with these rituals we simply try to give them a frame. (...) And we realise more and more that the children don't have this at home any more, that there are a lot of children who are alone in the afternoon, or who do not have any communication with other children in the afternoon. And, aahm, these rituals are in some way an exercise, to some extent, this is how we have it, how we use them." (GMS 02)

"I find rituals important. In my class, a ritual is that we have circle time quite often, or the morning-circle, or particular ways of doing things that are ritualised also. I find them important because (...) the children have a structure, and I realise again and again that it is only because of this that the children are functioning." (GMS 10)

Such views are not exclusive though to teachers in German mainstream schools. Orientation, structure, order are also present in the personal theories on rituals of teachers in free alternative schools.

"Well I, I believe for, aahm, for a school as ours it is quite important that there are rituals because there is so much freedom for children, they can decide on so many things, when where and what they want to do. And therefore it needs such, such basic rituals, to have something like a keystone, to give them orientation, you know." (FAS 02)

Rituals are also seen as a means to make life easier in school.

"For me rituals are re-occurring activities (..) that I (..) have negotiated, or so. In parts I have negotiated them, or else, that I also in parts do automatically, or, that for me are rituals. And in parts I do them quite consciously, simply because it is too exhausting otherwise, the whole thing. (...) We have them in our daily schedule, such rituals, that are meant to make life easier, partly also with the purpose for example to lead to independence, so, well, all sorts of rituals." (FAS 06)

One teacher from a mainstream school explains this aspect a bit more detailed in relation to children who take on a role of performing on stage in a weekly school-assembly. The assembly is interpreted as a ritual by her. The children on stage follow a fixed script.

"Yes, you get rid of having to make decisions constantly, do I attend assembly, do I not, what will I say when on stage, what not to say, you know. (...) It is anyway so exciting to stand on stage with a microphone in front of 250 people. If the children did not have this format, but rather had to make it up themselves every time, they would not do that any more. So it has something of relief, it has something liberating." (GMS 04)

In the same sense the idea of rituals as a means to generally simplify life in a social situation is also prevalent.

"In a school, in this habitat, this rather artificial habitat where, you know, 250 people live together, and so and so many adults, it needs a sort of economy, too. (...) An economy of energy, because that is all so exhausting, you know, you are together with so many people for the whole day. There are so many sensual impressions. And I believe, aahm, it is also necessary to find certain economic rituals, and if you have them and they match this perfectly, then they can remain like that for the time being." (GMS 04)

Furthermore the motif of rituals as having a meaning is brought up.

"Q – So you do have the term as a generic term in the school?

A – Yes, yes. And it is important to us. We find rituals important (...) well, rituals as activities that are virtually re-occurring in a particular and a fixed rhythm, activities that are, contain substance, and maybe also (...) meaning, at best." (FAS 11)

Where there is a lack of meaning perceived in an activity it consequently can call the term ritual for the activity into question. In relation to the regular excursion day once a week in one of the free alternative schools the teacher in the interview concludes that it is actually not a ritual.

"Yes, I wouldn't call it a ritual, but rather (...) well, what is it then, a fixed element comes to mind, I can't find the right word, but it goes into the direction of a ritual. But, nooo, a ritual is after all, it is something sacred. [laughs]" (FAS 10)

In thinking, or talking about rituals these teachers make use of "ready meanings [that] lie around." The dissemination of concepts of ritual via teacher training courses has been mentioned already. These 'ready meanings' are available also in form of the various articles in periodicals for teachers and their use as point of reference not the least also within teacher education. Four of the German teachers explicitly referred to experiences during their teacher training whereby they attended seminars on rituals.

There is no equivalent on the Irish side. Rituals in education are not a topic that would be represented by a coherent discussion within educational science in the English speaking world. So far it is not a topic in educational literature from Ireland, neither is it discussed in teacher education. Hence when Irish teachers are asked about the use of the term rituals in relation to their practice, they unanimously state that they do not use the term.

A teacher who was on secondment for part of her career: *"The term ritual or ritualisation, and I have worked in many schools in my previous career, I have never come across the term ritual or ritualisation. You know when I would be discussing, talking staff meetings or, ahm, yes, working with staffs on topics, it didn't come into their vocabulary or it wasn't." (IPS 02)*

This is confirmed also by other teachers.

"A - So, you're asking if I've ever heard of the word ritual being used with our, with our daily routines?

Q - Pretty much yes, does anybody use this term?

A - No. No.

Q - So in your, say in a staff meeting, or in a staff planning day, or even in your meetings with your colleague you would never use the term ritual for any of the activities that you reflect upon?

A - No, I've never heard of it been used, no." (IPS 06)

Instead of rituals the Irish teachers normally refer to re-occurring activities as routines.[13] The area in which they would identify the use of the term ritual as fitting is where it is about religious activities.

"You see, when you say ritual I kind of think it's a, I don't know what it is, I kind of think, well you always, you have religious ritual, I kind of think it's something major, like something like, you know, like a big thing that happens. You know like, here it's religious again, Christmas comes, ritual, you know, comes once a year. That kind, I'm not thinking of everyday, you know like, I mean, there's lots of stuff we do everyday. I

13 A very recent contribution on research about eating rituals in schools was made by Birgit Althans and Marc Tull, two German scholars, at the Ethnography and Education Conference, Oxford, September 2013. They also revert to a usage of the terms routine and ritual alongside to each other. This does not necessarily account for highest terminological clarity. However the partial blurring of terms probably seems feasible to make the main points of argument in their paper understandable for an English audience. (Althans/Tull 2013)

mean most things are done everyday, like, we call it again routine, not ritual." (IPS 01)

Or as expressed by another teacher in the interview:

"Q - Would you yourself use that term ritual or ritualisation? If you were talking to a colleague or a parent or to somebody else, would you use the term?

A - No, I definitely wouldn't. I don't know why, I don't know, is there nearly (...) not a negative, I don't know, I would never use that term.

Q - What would you use instead? You have described two different areas, one is the daily structure in the classroom ...

A - Yes, I suppose I would call that routine.

Q - That's routines?

A - Yes, I wouldn't call it, I wouldn't call it a ritual. As regards sort of things that happen in school as regards graduations and different things that they take part in, aahm, I try to think here how to describe that (...) tradition, I suppose in some sense of that word. That they're traditions to our school. I suppose even though I'm not sure if that's quite the right word. But in our school I suppose, yes, tradition is more a word.

Q - O.K., are there religious activities happening in the school also?

A - Yes.

Q - Things like morning prayer, confirmation preparation?

A - Morning prayer, confirmation, aahm, every year, so say third class goes to mass one Friday of the month, then the next Friday fourth goes to mass, and the next Friday fifth and sixth.

Q - And would you classify that as a ritual, too, or not?

A - I, yes, I suppose it is, yes. I suppose things like that carol service that we do every Christmas, actually we're quite, quite strongly involved in the church. There are quite a lot throughout the year." (IPS 07)

When teachers in Ireland think of activities that in a German context would be understood as ritual, they instead think of routines, traditions, but also of habits, celebrations, repeated procedures or simply repeated behaviour all of which were mentioned as terms in the interviews. In this regard the frequency and regularity of certain activities in school is acknowledged by the Irish teachers in the use of the term routine. It is also clear that such activities can be done in an automated fashion. They become *"part and parcel"* (IPS 08) of the daily activities.

If we look at the "ready meanings that lie around" thus for the Irish teachers they are not exactly the same as for the German teachers. A dissemination of a debate on rituals within Ireland similar to Germany is missing. Teachers in Ireland consequently don't talk or think about their practice in terms of ritual. They yet have their personal theories of rituals. In these the Irish teachers regularly associate the term with religion, but there is also an awareness of a shortcoming in a purely religious understanding of the term.

"I suppose the difficulty lies with the use of the term ritual because it is so often associated with religious ritual. Ahm, it's rarely used outside of that. Routine is used. But there are things that are not religious, have no religious connotations, are they rituals? And, yes, I'd say they are." (IPS 02)

In the interviews with the Irish teachers it is however also a regular occurrence that they accommodate for the use of the term ritual during the actual interview. While at the one side they don't use the term when talking about their practice, they are still familiar with the term as such. It is not the case that ritual would be a word they have never heard. In fact during the interviews they readily apply the term to activities that they otherwise would depict as routines.

"A - O.K. It's not a term that I've used. I suppose meeting and greeting visitors or other teachers the children in any school get in to the habit of greeting the, maybe as a whole group, in some schools the whole class stands up and says 'Dia duit, tá fáilte romhat' whatever or 'Good morning, you're welcome.' Is that, I'm asking this of myself, is that a ritual? Maybe.

Q - If you think along the line of this being a ritual, what would be the reason for you to classify that as a ritual?

A - Because it's done with frequency and almost without thinking. It's an automated kind of response that when a visitor comes in the children would, I know from visiting schools that, visiting different classrooms, that would be one that would stand out. Children would stand up and say 'good morning teacher' or." (IPS 02)

What stands out as difference between teachers in Germany and teachers in Ireland is first of all the apparent confidence and the familiarity with concepts and terminology of German teachers when talking about rituals in school. German teachers in speaking about ritual tap into a source of thoughts that appear to be in a certain way coherent. They consequently have a personal theory of ritual that is sufficient to make them confident enough to speak about their practice in terms of ritual. This is not to say anything about the quality or stringency of these personal theories. In fact these are often "common sense theories (…) not a conscious and elaborate theory", but rather "replicas of (...) theories that have woven their way into the fabric of everyday consciousness" (Haug 1999).

Secondly however there is the particular line of argument that is prevalent in the German discourse where rituals are positively perceived as providing safety, reliability and structure to children and the grounding of such an idea in children's needs. Such a connection does not feature with the Irish teachers.

I have pointed to the character of this line of argument as a killer-phrase that can be strategically used to prevent any (further) critical questioning. The proliferation of this motif in Germany is probably best illustrated by the comments of one of the teachers from a free alternative school who has personal experiences with schools in England. From her experience within the school community of the free alternative school she concludes that rituals and ritualistic activities are seen as important for teachers and parents alike.

"Ahm, and it is seen, and I feel like that is seen as very important, certainly like the parent community hold this need of ritual, this idea that the students, that the children need these rituals, these sort of ritualistic activity, that it happens at that time every day and it's done in this way (...) That I think is where I have a different, I feel like this ritualistic part that here is really much more extreme than in England.[14] *Like, the, how*

14 This is not to suggest that there are less or no rituals in schools in England. Similarly it does not mean that in an English speaking context, discussions about children's needs would be absent. The anchoring of the arguments for having rituals in the 'needs of children' however is a specific German phenomenon.

important that is, like it almost, to me it always seems, ahm, artificial, something. And parents absolutely and the team as well very: 'This is important, this is what the children need.'" (FAS 09)

3.3. Ritual Cultures in Different School Types

From the material gathered in the interview series it is possible to also generate a comparative overview of those activities that teachers in the three different school types see as rituals. The various activities can be sorted into a number of areas according to thematic coherence. They shall be presented here in a table format first.

There are two points of caution to be made about this overview. The first concerns the number of primary sources (interviews) that are used as the basis for it. It is possible that a survey on a bigger scale may lead to adjustments in relation to certain activities as listed above. The list of activities may also be extended if a bigger number of teachers were included in a survey. However the experience in a workshop at the national conference of the free alternative schools suggests that the list presented here is quite comprehensive already. In the workshop 28 people from different schools did a brainstorming on rituals in their schools and the collected activities at that time did not contain any activity that is not yet included in the table overview also.

Therefore in some cases the ratios may not be as accurate as they would be if the number of informants was increased. In spite of these restrictions the table still proves valuable in relation to identifying general tendencies within the three school types.

The second point of caution is to repeat that the activities mentioned are *perceived* as rituals by the teachers. This is not to say that these activities *are* rituals. As shown in the first chapter there are multiple ways to classify activities for their qualities to be ritual or not. For these teachers based on their *personal theories* however it is appropriate to speak of them as rituals.

Activities mentioned in interviews as rituals in different school types; total number of interviews: FAS (14), GMS (12), IPS (9)				
Theme	Activity	FAS	GMS	IPS
(Self-) Governance	Morning circle, end of day circle[15]	18	17	2
	School assembly / Class Council	9	4	0
	Juridical Committee	1	0	0
	Anti-violence-committee	0	1	0
	Booklet for messages to parents	0	1	0
	Staff meeting	1	1	0
Administration	Writing annual reports	1	0	0
	Attendance check	1	1	0
	Meeting school inspector	1	0	0
Reverence	Religious activities, prayers, mass	0	1	8
	National anthem at end of school day	0	0	1
Calender Rituals	Celebrations (Summer, Christmas, Solstice ...)	8	6	1
Celebration of Growth - Rites of Passage	First day of school	6	2	0
	Birthday	4	3	0
	Farewell celebration for school leavers	4	1	0
	Transition primary to secondary section in same school	3	0	0
Celebration of Achievements	Award Ceremonies	0	0	3
Annual Activities	Annual Sports Day	0	1	1
	Reading night	0	1	0
	School trips	3	0	0
	Overnight stay in school	1	0	0
	Boys/Girls-day	1	0	0

15 Some teachers mentioned more than one circle (e. g. morning-circle, story-circle, circle time to solve conflicts).

Theme	Activity	FAS	GMS	IPS
Time-tabling	Scheduled activities during regular school time (e. g. reading time, swimming lessons)	6	3	3
	Project-week	0	2	0
Internal Performances	Open stage	1	0	0
	Dance performance	0	1	0
Structuring Lessons	Everyday routines in lessons (e.g. diary entries, homework check)	0	7	6
Housekeeping	Tidying up (Classrooms, Yard)	2	4	0
Meals	Meals (Breakfast/Lunch)	5	3	2
Status Confirmation	Welcome formulas (class greets teacher – teacher greets class)	0	5	1
Behaviour Management	Non-verbal communication (e.g. 'sound-bowl', raising hand to get silence in class, rain-stick) for 'managing behaviour'	0	7	0[16]
	Chatting up children in bus	0	0	1
	'Rules for good listening' – verbal instruction, mantra	0	0	1
Symbolic Gratification or Punishment	Stickers, smileys, 'traffic light'-classroom-management-system, presentation of certificates	0	7	2
Regulating Group Physical Order	Lining up after break time	0	4	6
	Dismissal (order of classes to go)	0	0	1
	Change of seating order in regular time intervals	0	1	1

The symbolic and expressive character of rituals was mentioned already. Taking rituals as indicators they are carriers of information about the norms, values, beliefs that are characteristic for the school in which they appear. It is also possible that within one school not all rituals necessarily represent the same values. This line of thought shall be

16 One of the teachers in the Irish interview series mentioned that she does raise hands to get silence – but she does not see this as a ritual, for her it is merely a technique.

picked up soon again. First however a few words on some of the thematic areas listed in the table.

Circle Time / (Self-)Governance

Circle time is the one activity that in German schools, be they mainstream or free alternative schools, is seen as a ritual by nearly everyone (and in some cases even mentioned more than once by the same teacher depicting different circles). However it is important to note that circle time in free alternative school and circle time in a mainstream school are not necessarily the same thing.

Birgit Althans/Michael Göhlich (2004, pp. 215 – 219) have highlighted differences in the structure of communication in circle time in different schools. The communitarian morning assembly around a large breakfast table in the Free School Frankfurt offers quite different ways of relating to each other than the circle time in a mainstream school where the teacher determines who speaks at what time and on what topic. The most thing that circle time in all schools has in common is the idea of the actual shape: a circle.

The spatial distribution of bodies in a circle is also an ideological statement. The circle evokes the idea of egalitarian participation. There is no front or back, top or bottom in a circle. Circle time stands out as *the ritual* in German schools. The message sent out on the level of appearance however does not necessarily coincide with the character of the relationships. This is particularly the case for German mainstream schools.

School meetings (assemblies) are a frequent occurrence in free alternative schools. These meetings are normally decision-making forums. Often school rules are discussed in these meetings in which children and adults take part.

For German mainstream schools 'class-council' is a propagated as a way to "develop a democratic culture" in the school. It is painted as "a time slot in which the class can discuss in a democratic and self-responsible form all those ongoing topics that are of concern for the class and the pupils. In class-council teachers and pupils are partners with equal rights" (Daublebsky/Lauble 2006, p. 7).

It is a somehow naïve construction to assume that teachers and pupils in mainstream schools are partners with equal rights. Their position from the very start of their being teacher or pupil is one that is based on a status difference. The rights of teachers to regulate the business of pupils is clearly laid out in school law. Attempts of teachers in these circumstances to establish decision making structures in their classroom that are truly egalitarian will always be made in contrast to the conditions on which they are actually teachers in these classrooms.

Stephan Münte-Goussar in his critical analysis of reform pedagogy points to the ambiguity inherent in applying methods like class-council within a school whose practice is based on set targets. “In general terms the aim is to renounce frontal instruction and reduce the centrality of the teacher: cutting back all those forms in which the teacher is the visible and constantly acting agent who delivers content, monitors targets, steers and organises the instructional arrangements. (…) The nature of the targets and the time-line for reaching them may be the same for everyone or it may be individualised for each child. (…) The structure of target orientation is the same in both cases. Decentralising the role of the teacher does not change this” (Münte-Goussar 2001, pp. 50/51). Teachers still remain in a position of responsibility for maintaining a structure of instruction that guarantees that the targets are reached.

With the exception of two cases in which teachers mention circle time in their interviews there is no other reference made by Irish teachers to activities that could be subsumed under (self-)governance. This is at odds with the results of a survey published by the National Council for Curriculum and Assessment 2008 in which 49 % of participating teachers reported to use circle time “frequently”, and another 32 % reported to use it “sometimes” (NCCA 2008, p. 79). Bernie Collins has pointed to significant uncertainties in relation to these figures. In her work on circle time in Irish primary schools she notes that “these figures may not fully reflect classroom reality” (Collins 2011, p. 81).

Nevertheless there are attempts to raise awareness of issues like children's voice and participation in primary school in Ireland. The promotion of circle time in teacher education and continuing professional development can be seen as such an attempt. Obviously in promoting circle time in these environments it is yet not depicted as a ritual, as would frequently be the case in German teacher education.

Another prominent approach in this line is also the pus[illegible]
councils to be established on primary level. Owen McLoughli[illegible]
an exemplary account of such an initiative in a Dublin primar[illegible]
(McLoughlin 2005). However these discussion are at a stage whe[illegible]
only filter through very slowly into the practice of Irish nat[illegible]
schools.[17]

Reverence

It is of little surprise to see religious activities being mentioned as examples of ritual activities in Irish primary schools. As we have seen in the understanding of Irish teachers of the actual notion of ritual is strongly associated with the realm of religion. Furthermore the fact that 96 % of all Irish schools are under the patronage of either the catholic or the protestant church suggests that religious activities are widespread in Irish primary education.

German mainstream schools in contrast are under states patronage and thus separated from the church. The free alternative schools equally have no religious agenda.[18] Consequently there is no mentioning of religious activities as rituals in these schools.

Calendar Celebrations / Rites of Passage

While religious activities are separated from the actual school practice in Germany, there are yet other activities that fulfil similar functions. In his work on the elementary forms of religious life Emile Durkheim has used the term collective effervescence for the experience of emotionally charged human inter-subjectivity (Durkheim 1915/1926, pp. 215 ff). This emotional charge can be achieved by participating in social gatherings irrespective of their particular framing. The calendar celebrations that take place in German schools can be seen to fulfil this function. Historically carnival, winter-solstice or summer-festival may have links

17 An indicator of the current state of affairs in this regard is the statement of Tralee Educate Together National School on their webpage in which it says: " We are proud to be the only primary school in Kerry to have a Student Council at primary level." (http://www.tralee-educate-together.com/student-council.html [15. 07. 2012])

18 For accuracy it should be mentioned that there is one of the FAS where religious motifs are explicitly included in the school concept.

celebration in the context of German schools is religious terms.

ssage mentioned by the teachers as prevalent in ir focal point in school itself. The first day of amilies is as big an event as Holy Communion Kellermann 2008).

cluded birthday celebrations in this section. chool they can be interpreted as a rite that lies at the point ersection between natural growth (calendar) and institutional status progress (passage). As a rite that refers back to the individual life history it brings the family as alternative institution back to mind, thus transcending the institutional life span and pointing to the individuality of the child as being more than just a pupil. At the same time the actual choreography of birthday celebrations in schools can counter this reminder again and turn the ritual into an affirmation of the child's status of being a pupil (see e. g. Piper 1997, pp. 225 – 240).

Time-tabling

Time-tabling of activities is seen as ritual by teachers in all three school types. This refers back to the initial definition of rituals as re-occurring activities.

Despite the fact that children in free alternative schools are generally free to choose if they wish to participate in an activity, there is normally a clear time structure in these schools, too. Certain activities are scheduled for certain times and spaces (rooms). This can include sessions in which a particular subject is dealt with, e. g. if a part time English teacher is only available on Wednesday morning or the weekly swimming session in the local pool that can be booked only for Thursday afternoon.

When teachers mention time-tabling as a ritualistic element they however also refer to the time-structure of the school days or school week as such, e. g. lunch time, assemblies.

Lesson Structuring

A ritualistic structure of lessons is depicted only in mainstream schools, that is Irish and German mainstream schools alike. Teachers of free alternative schools don't refer to lesson structuring in terms of ritual.

This makes sense if one remembers that the children in free alternative schools normally choose to take part in a session, that the guiding principle is mathetic instead of didactic, that this implies that learning is an inquiry rather than an instruction (even where it happens in an interactive situation with one partner taking on a teaching role), that the groups that are together for a session are normally rather small and certainly never count 25 plus as can be the case in mainstream schools, that elements like homework and continuous assessment are alien to free alternative schools.

The formality of traditional instruction is abandoned in this environment. The term lesson itself is hardly applicable for the learning activities that go on in free alternative schools (see: Scholz 1996, pp. 114 – 159). On this basis teachers in free alternative schools don't mention activities that would be similar to those identified as lesson structuring by their counterparts in mainstream schools.

Status Confirmation / Behaviour Management / Symbolic Gratification / Group Order

These four areas are all not represented in the free alternative schools. The simple reason for this is that they are practically absent in these schools.

Welcome formulas are reported as rituals by teachers in German mainstream schools. This refers to various aesthetics. Practices like holding hands in a circle stand beside those where the children of a class stand up from their seats to greet the teacher with a choral, "Good morning, Mrs/Mr X."

As much as there are no such welcome formulas the idea of behaviour management or classroom management is also alien to free alternative schools. It clashes diametrically with a culture of negotiation where teachers can't claim authority qua status.

In mainstream schools however this area is a constant topic for teachers. The plethora of articles that is available on classroom management and behaviour management documents this quite strikingly. The bottom line in all approaches of managing behaviour (or classroom management which is essentially managing behaviour in the classroom) is that there is a divide between teacher and pupil. The one manages the other, not vice versa.

It is also assumed that this actually works, which in fact it does with some children, but not with others. "Adult-child power relations are constituted, learned and understood through the embodied restriction of movement within space and control of various elements of power, such as noise, knowledge, and access to material objects, and manipulative use of popularity and status attached to physical and mental ability" (Gore 2004, p. 59).

Techniques of managing behaviour include the use of symbolic gratification or punishment (smileys, stickers) or the regulation of movement (lining up, seating order).[19] Teachers in mainstream school refer to these elements of their practice as rituals.

A particular aspect that is prevalent in German mainstream schools, but not (yet) in Irish primary schools is also the use of non-verbal communication. As we have seen in the chapter on rituals "ritualisation is simultaneously the avoidance of explicit speech and narrative" (Bell 1992, p. 111). Ingrid Kellermann's catalogue of potential behaviour for a teacher in disciplining rituals contained fleeting gestures, symbolic body language, specific mimic and gestures (Kellermann 2008, p. 216). The use of acoustic devices is also part of the repertoire of mainstream teachers in Germany to manage children's behaviour.

"There have been two classes 6 and 7, which became more and more impatient, aggressive (…) The reason was in both cases the increase of pressure to perform, the discontinuity of rituals and abilities from primary school; classes with a 'normal' development in an integrated comprehensive school, where usually (...) the weaker students simply

19 The regulation of movement is essentially an attempt of controlling the bodily expressions of others. How to legitimately use one's body in an educational environment is also at the core of discussions about teacher conduct. In the context of the discourse on child abuse/child protection this plays a significant role (see e.g. Jones 2001, or also: Langer 2008).

drop out mentally and find substitutes of satisfaction in aggressive behaviour (…) struggles with teachers or acts of shoplifting in the nearby supermarket, while the better students become individual fighters. (…) I badly needed silence in the classes. Practising silence, how to do this? (…) I decided to try out the rain-stick (…) We started the lesson in a totally different way. All students were asked to become completely silent (…) *'Now all of you, please listen and imagine a picture to what you hear,'* was the instruction and I took the little rain-stick out of my pocket. Slowly the sand fell, an everlasting, endless and fascinatingly calm sound (…) For three minutes I let the rain-stick sound, five minutes passed with the whole exercise ongoing. [Afterwards] the class remained very calm, the children put up their hands to talk, listened to and did not interrupt each other or made noise. (…) Obviously I used the topic for the art lessons and the children painted pictures about 'Silence and Calmness'" (Büttner 1996, p. 7).

It is worth noting that the requested behaviour is almost at all times to be quiet, to move slowly, to keep hands still, to look at the teacher, etc., hence: restrictive demands. In this regard Irish primary schools don't differ from the German mainstream schools. A good example for this are the "rules for good listening" that are promoted via colourful posters. The first time I came across such a poster was in a classroom of a second class in a multi-denominational school in Ireland in 2008. It shows a smiling child sitting behind a desk with hands folded and legs tightly kept together. The text on the poster states: Eyes are watching. Ears are listening. Lips are closed. Hands are still. Feet are quiet. There are lines drawn from the written sentences to the corresponding body parts of the child. The poster is kept in strong colours with a bright yellow background, the t-shirt of the child in strong red. The colourful display does not change the disciplining and restrictive character of the demand put on children.

In the interview series a teacher referred to her applying the rules of good listening as an "attention ritual": *"Sometimes I, I know some teachers at the beginning of every lesson, you know, have a, an attention ritual where they have bums on seat, you know, feet on the ground, hands are still, eyes are watching, ears are listening, brainbox is on. That's I think a little attention ritual that some teachers do. And I do it sometimes during my class." (IPS 06)*

Similarities and Differences

Comparing the three different school types according to the rituals reported by the teachers in the interview series we find similarities and divisions. Taking rituals as indicators for the norms, values, beliefs that are constitutional for a school the situation within German mainstream schools appears to be the least clear.

Teachers of all three school types mention time-tabling, the re-occurrence of activities at scheduled times as ritual elements in their practice.

Irish teachers identify rituals in their schools first and foremost in the area of religious activities. However in merging notions of ritual and routines they also report of elements of lesson structuring and regulating group physical order.

Teachers from free alternative schools don't mention rituals in relation to instruction (lesson structuring), regulation of bodies in space, symbolic gratification or status confirmation at all. Instead they refer to rites of passage, to calendar rites and particularly to rituals of (self-)governance.

Teachers from German mainstream schools include in their reports calender rites, rituals relating to instruction (lesson structuring), to regulation of bodies in space, to symbolic gratification, but at the same time rituals of (self-)governance.

The collection of rituals derived for Irish primary schools and the one for free alternative schools evokes the impression of a set of activities that are rather coherent in their own contexts. Albeit coming from two completely different sides, both of these school types provide an environment in which a rather consistent system of values, norms, beliefs finds itself expressed, enacted and thereby continuously reshaped according to the dynamics of negotiations within the schools.

German mainstream schools in contrast can be depicted as an environment in which the ritual culture indicates a situation in which contradictory value systems, norms, beliefs are represented in the daily practice of the schools.

Authority, hierarchy, discipline are the topics that are addressed differently in the three school types. The ambiguity of the teacher's role in German mainstream schools in this sense is certainly higher than it is for teachers in free alternative schools or in Irish primary schools. Obviously what we find here is a momentary picture which can change over time. At this stage of history it is a fair guess to assume that in particular the situation in the Irish schools will change in the future. In Irish society the system of religious patronage is more and more seen as anachronistic. The influx of migration from within the European Union and beyond is felt particularly in the urban areas. The effects of these developments are likely to filter through to all areas of social life. Having more and more children from families with differing value systems, norms, beliefs in a school will make it more difficult to present values, norms, beliefs in a consistent manner.

Taking German mainstream schools as a point of departure in the next section I will attend to the ambiguous symbolic representations as observed in two rituals in school: circle time and line of pairs.

3.4. Ambiguous Symbolic Representations - Circle and Line

As described in chapter one rituals are commonly seen as symbolically representing values, norms, beliefs, the social order of the respective social system in which they are enacted. Here now I am going to look at symbolic representations that can be observed in circle time and lining up as two distinct school rituals.

Lining up in pairs is a practice in schools all over the globe. One can find it in Japan, in South America, in the United States as well as in Australia. You can meet children in a line of pairs in a park in London, in Dublin's suburbs on the way to a football field, in the most rural west of Ireland walking from school to church. There is even an informal term in the English language for such a line of schoolchildren walking in pairs. It is called the crocodile.

Underlying this practice is a proto-typical model. The pairs, while moving, keep a definite distance one person to the other as well as pair to pair in the row. Every single person has got a fixed position in a grid formation. This position can be named accurately in a numeric series: first left, third right, fourth left etc. Yet the phenomenon is completely described only if we mention those persons, who accompany the formation, in our case the teachers. They don't integrate themselves into the close formation. If there are two, they usually are one in front and one at the back. Normally these persons determine direction and speed of the group and they are an integral part of the entire ensemble.

In my earlier analysis of the line of pairs (Hamm 1999) I have used the toolbox of Michel Foucault to describe some characteristics of this formation. In *Discipline & Punish*, a historical study about the penal system, Foucault analyses power relations in society, their mechanisms and results. While Foucault takes the prison as the starting point of his research, the patterns and principles he identifies there are also prevalent in hospital, workhouse, school and military barracks. Foucault speaks of a policy of coercions which was applied in these institutions. At the centre of these policies was the body of the prisoner, the inmate, the pupil. The human sciences (medicine, psychiatry, pedagogy) helped to establish a regime "over others' bodies, not only so they may do what one wishes, but so that they may operate as one wishes, with the techniques, the speed and the efficiency that one determines" (Foucault 1995; p. 138). Which are the procedures, instruments, the techniques that we find in use in our case? With the help of Foucault we can identify: the art of distributions, the control of activity, the composition of forces, the hierarchical observation and the normalising judgement.[20]

The Art of Distributions

In the disciplinary institution the distribution of individuals is of utmost importance. Of particular interest in our context is the cellular structure of partitioning. "Disciplinary space tends to be divided into as many sections as there are bodies or elements to be distributed. One must eliminate the effects of imprecise distributions, the uncontrolled disappearance of individuals, their diffuse circulation, their unusable and dangerous coagulation; (…) establish presences and absences, to know where and how to locate the individuals, to set up useful communications, to interrupt others (…)." What else would be lining up

20 There are two other elements identified by Foucault: the organisation of geneses; the examination. They are certainly detectable in schools, but for the particular ritual of lining up they don't play a central role.

in pairs if not distributing individuals in a *'tableaux vivants'*, partitioning the entire group by the principle of elementary location: “Each individual has its own place; and each place its individual” (Foucault 1995, p. 143).

The Control of Activity

In the ideal formation this is the rhythm in which the individuals are marching in step. Obviously the degree to which this is implemented differs with the various institutional backgrounds. For the children in school it is yet clear that they walk when they are told to walk, they stand when they are told to stand.

The Composition of Forces

At the same time as the bodies in the formation are made identifiable in their cellular positioning, they are also integrated into a whole ensemble. The individual child becomes a body-segment of the crocodile. This impression is even stronger where the children are also wearing school uniforms, thereby planishing even the visual differences of appearance amongst them to the minimum.

The Hierarchical Observation

Without surveillance the disciplinary authority is fragile. Foucault pays some attention to the architectural design of the institutions in which the hierarchical observation is built into the arrangement of walls, windows, doors and corridors. "Latrines had been installed with half-doors, so that the supervisor on duty could see the head and legs of the pupils, and also with side walls sufficiently high 'that those inside cannot see another'. This infinitely scrupulous concern with surveillance is expressed in the architecture by innumerable petty mechanisms. These mechanisms can only be seen as unimportant if one forgets the role of this instrumentation, minor but flawless, in the progressive objectification and the ever more subtle partitioning of individual behaviour. The disciplinary institutions secreted a machinery of control that functioned like a microscope of conduct ..." (Foucault 1995, p. 173).

Outside the school building however there is nothing more obvious than the surveillance. It is guaranteed simply by the guarding adults positioned in front and behind the group. They are essential part of the whole ensemble.

Observation aims to control behaviour, gestures, activities, movements. Though the final target of discipline is more than the gesture, in the first instance its grip is exactly here. If non-conform and deviant behaviour emerges, it will be penalised. Foucault identifies at the heart of the disciplinary systems the functioning of a "small penal mechanism. It enjoys a kind of judicial privilege, with its own laws, its specific offences, its particular forms of judgement. The disciplines established an 'infra-penality', they partitioned an area that the laws had left empty; they defined and repressed a mass of behaviour that the relative indifference of the great systems of punishment had allowed to escape" (Foucault 1995, p. 178).

We can hear the teacher: "Line up! Hold Andrew's hand! Don't turn while walking! Stay in line!" And if someone is walking one foot on the pavement, the other on the street: "You will get some extra work to do!"

The judgements in disciplinary institutions are ideally turned into a task for the perpetrator to realise the propagated purposes of the institution in form of intensified or specialised practice. Foucault notes that alongside "punishments borrowed directly from the judicial model (fines, flogging, solitary confinement), the disciplinary systems favour punishments that are exercise – intensified, mulitpled forms of training, several times repeated" (Foucault 1995, p. 179).

An example found in John Burningham's fabulous book about John Patrick Norman McHennessy, a boy who always comes late to school (1987):

"John Patrick Norman McHennessy set off along the road to learn. On the way a crocodile came out of the drain and got hold of his satchel. John Patrick Norman McHennessy pulled and pulled but the crocodile would not let go. He threw a glove into the air and the crocodile snapped at the glove and let go of the satchel. John Patrick Norman McHennessy hurried along the road to learn but the crocodile had made him late.

'John Patrick Norman McHennessy, you are late and where is your other glove?'

'I am late, Sir, because on the way a crocodile came out of a drain and got hold of my satchel, and would only let go when I threw my glove, which he ate.'

'There are no crocodiles living in drains around here. You are to stay in late and write out 300 times, *I must not tell lies about crocodiles and I must not lose my glove*.'

So John Patrick Norman McHennessy stayed in late and wrote out 300 times, *I must not tell lies about crocodiles and I must not lose my glove*."

*

While circle time is a relatively new feature in mainstream schools, the line of pairs is not. It is a fully established practice. However it had to be established at some stage in history, too. In the first part of the 19th century Carl Zerrenner was a school inspector in Prussia. He published extensively on manifold aspects of schooling. Many of his texts specifically addressed teacher seminars. In one of them he recommends:

"In many schools, when letting the students out of the classrooms into the break on the yard, you should let go one class after the other and form each class one bench behind the next – the teacher following the last student. This is necessary in particular where classes are in an upper floor and students have to make their way using the stairs. How quick an accident might happen there! After being restricted for a time and now for moments permitted freedom in particular boys tend to mischievous and rough behaviour. The same attention must be given at the end of the lessons when the students leave the school. If the minutes of recreation are over, again in many schools for safety reasons the classes have to return separately to the classrooms. For boys in the moment of the school bell ringing it is most advantageous to establish a certain order in which the boys of each class are standing in pairs behind each other without moving until the teacher steps forward and commands them into the classroom. The military in the procedure is a pleasure for the boys and it prevents lots of mischief and accidents, especially if the classrooms are in the upper floors. On several occasions I have seen that teachers are utilizing this manoeuvre for a control of students dress and cleanliness of hands and more" (Zerrenner 1826, p. 82).

The basic assumption underlying the recommendations of Carl Zerrenner is also clearly stated: "All morality of children in the first instance emerges as obedience. It can only develop as the result of effective school discipline, teaching alone is not sufficient. And, is not all the essence of virtue found in order and regularity? Do we not have to force already children to obey?" (Zerrenner 1826, p. 9).

It is quite obvious that the patterns which we find in the line of pairs are hardly symbolic of self-responsibility, self-esteem, equality, or other attributes that are fashion in present day pedagogy. They are rather closely linked to the subordination of the early days of pedagogical treatment, rooted in a military aesthetic, aiming at order, regularity, obedience as its highest achievement.

The ritual practice symbolically represents these values and the corresponding norms. At the same time each individual performance of the ritual reaffirms them. In the constant repetition of the ritual the values and norms are materially enacted, they become real. The Berlin ritual studies have extensively highlighted the mimetic aspects of rituals and their consequences for the material performances. Due to these aspects a line of pairs in one school can look different to that in another one, a line of pairs in a particular school can look different today than it did ten years ago or during the 1950's.

For all variations in appearance it is yet the case that they still enact a pattern that is structured on the military model depicted by Carl Zerrenner. The legacy of this model can not be shaken off, it is essential to the line of pairs, just as the underlying construction of virtue found in forging children into obedient creatures. The proto-typical child in the line of pairs is anything but self-responsible, the relationships expressed are anything than egalitarian. This is obviously at odds with contemporarily stated pedagogical targets. Circle time seems to be much better suited to express those.

From Michel Foucault we can learn that it is not the first time, that the circle is state of the art. He describes the architectural figure of the Panopticum, designed by Jeremy Bentham at the end of the 18th century as the ideal prison. This is a building circular in shape like a ring with open space in the centre. In the centre a tower is placed with windows facing the inner side of the ring. In the building at the periphery there are cells that span the entire width of the building. There is a window to the outside and one to the inside of the building in each cell. Thus the light can cross through the cell. From the position in the tower it is possible to monitor what is going on in each cell. At the same time it is not possible to see from the cell into the tower. The Panopticon is like "a machine for dissociating the see/being seen dyad: in the peripheric ring, one is totally seen, without ever seeing; in the central tower, one sees everything without ever being seen" (Foucault 1995, p. 200).

The idea of seeing without being seen is still quite prominent in many social fields. The development of technical equipment of surveillance, either visual or acoustic has reached quite utopian dimensions since the times of Jeremy Bentham. It is no longer necessary to construct the Panopticon by concrete, stone and glass, if it is much easier installed in any architecture by using simple cable strings. CCTV, tracking via mobile phones, surveillance of communication via e-mail, internet could not even be dreamt of then.

Modern pedagogy however aims to create a somehow different effect by establishing the circular order. Circle time is not about dissociating the seeing/being seen dyad, it is rather aiming at the permanent mutual control that is dependent on the reciprocal relation of seeing/being seen.

Circle time is first of all a physical arrangement of bodies in space. In the last section a number of comments on circle time were made already. The shape of the circle contains an ideological statement. It is possible to find this clearly stated in conceptual papers also: "As symbolized by the shape of the circle here we have the equal right for every child to express thoughts, to express personality, to take initiative in front of a group. This is the place of social experience. The efforts of work are reflected. Usually the children determine the subjects. For the teachers, who generally stay in the background, this is the chance to evaluate speed and method of teaching as well as getting new ideas" (Eltern-Kind-Initiative 1997, p. 25). Similar ideas expressed in an English speaking context: "The very act of sitting in a circle emphasises unity and equality, encouraging attitudes of honesty and trust. Taking it in turn to speak and join in the activities clearly conveys a message of authority and control to all participants" (Mosley 2004, p. 10).

Any physical arrangement of bodies in space has communicative value in itself. It is a statement conveying a message about the character of the particular assemblage of persons.

Due to our human make-up there is for us always a front and a back in relation to space. When Carl Zerrener refers to the "military in the procedure" of the line of pairs there is implicated also the creation of a front and a back. The line of pairs has a direction. In the aggregation each single body is facing the same way. Hence the attention and forces are bundled and straightly aligned. For the teachers taking a position outside of the grid formation clearly demonstrates their status. In the actual performance it is also made clear that the unit as a whole is at their disposal. This also means that a change of direction is possible at the will of the teacher. When walking: "Forward, march. To the left, march. etc." When standing: "Right face. Left face."

The direction of the circle is different. Here the aggregation brings the bodies in a shape that is focussing at a mid-point. The back is located in all directions at the outside. The front however is inside the circle. This is the only direction possible.[21] It can not be changed without dissolving the effect of the aggregation. The attention and forces of participants of the circle gear towards the centre and they are contained within the formation. For teachers it is essential to integrate.

At the same time circle-time is just as much about elimination of "imprecise distributions, the uncontrolled disappearance of individuals, their diffuse circulation, their unusable and dangerous coagulation; (…) establish presences and absences, to know where and how to locate the individuals, to set up useful communications, to interrupt others (…)."

Just like the line of pairs circle time is also a sequence of acts. The line of pairs is enacted by activities like standing, marching, stopping, walking (on the side of the children) and commanding, observing, standing, marching, stopping, walking (on the side of the adults). During circle time the activities are mainly sitting and talking. Effectively circle time is a ritual that is at the same time a game of speech.

21 It could be argued that the circle can be turned inside out in which case nobody sees anyone else and the back is in the mid-point while the front is located in all directions on the outside. This however is never done in practice.

Birgit Althans and Michael Göhlich have provided an example of circle time in fourth class in a mainstream primary school in Berlin. Here on Monday morning at the beginning of the school day all children come to sit in a circle on their chairs. The teacher takes up a little ball that lies on her desk. Then she says: "Now, as usual, let us tell each other what happened at the weekend." A few children lift their arms signalling that they would like to speak. The teacher throws the ball to a boy. The child tells what happened to him on Saturday. When he finishes the teacher reaches out with her hand for the ball and the child throws back the ball. Again a number of children lift their arms. She throws the ball to another child. And again, after finishing the child throws back the ball. Then the teacher gives the ball to a girl but stops her from starting to talk. Instead she addresses the whole class and says that it is too loud in the circle. Then the girl is allowed to speak. Afterwards the teacher gets back the ball. She now hands it over to another girl. Other children in the circle talk to each other increasingly loud. The teacher cautions the class and says that the purpose of the circle time is that they learn to listen to each other. She throws the ball to another child. The child talks. Afterwards the child throws back the ball to the teacher. Now the teacher speaks to the class and says: "When you tell everybody about your weekend quite often no-one can follow what you say. You need to think about what you want to tell in advance. You need to concentrate on one thing only." With that she concludes the round of telling stories from the weekend. Afterwards she announces information on the upcoming school tour and the parents meeting in relation to it. She answers question on this issue and eventually closes the circle time by saying: "Everyone goes back with their chair to their own table now" (Althans/Göhlich 2004, p. 218).

Althans/Göhlich see in this an example of teacher-centred instruction on speaking practice. They point out that in it the traditional dialogic interaction between teacher and pupils is seamlessly amalgamated with the ritual form of the circle. There can be no error made in locating authority and control in the situation clearly on the side of the teacher. Hence the symbolic representation of equality ascribed to the circle is one that only applies to the children amongst themselves. The traditional values, norms, beliefs that are constitutive for the role definition of teacher vs. pupil are in fact reaffirmed in this procedure, albeit in a new appearance.

One may argue that the teacher in this example provides a rather clumsy example of conducting circle time. It is yet a fact that even where teachers are more accustomed to the modern version of the game of speech, thus allowing them to “generally stay in the background,” the actual execution of circle time in school depends on the teacher initiating and maintaining it. Where children take ownership of the ritual it will normally be a sort of mock-ownership that is let go fast enough once the teacher does not provide the necessary scaffolding.

Yet for circle time, as long as the teacher guarantees for the ritual to happen, the ritualised and constantly repeated acknowledgement of values, norms of the institution is even more effective as it is exercised under the impression of participation and influence on the side of the children. And to keep dangerous tendencies at bay "the teachers who generally stay in the background" will no longer stay there if the generously awarded freedom could be used to establish other values, norms. An example that I witnessed when I visited a school for a day in Germany:

After the break the class comes together for circle time. They discuss an incident of disobedience. In the last week a boy had been throwing little wooden blocks in the play area. Therefore he was refused permission to play in the area for one week. On Thursday of this week was playing in the area together with two friends. The teacher brings the topic into the circle for decision. In the following discussion the children find, it is Thursday already and the boy obviously has not again thrown blocks. He rather played with his mates without any problem. For the children a dismissal of the previous judgement seems reasonable. At this point of discussion the teacher comes in. Referring to a more general level he states, such a decision could invite everyone to disobey every rule. Some pupils translate his seemingly neutral statement into the form of an appeal for another punishment of the boy. That eventually results in the repeated prohibition to play in the area for the boy.

This teacher is surely more skilful in playing the game of speech. Bernie Collins describes the role of teachers during circle-time as facilitative or 'counselling lite' (Collins 2011). The teacher in this example knows that ideally he has to avoid command or order. Instead he has to make suggestions, express opinions and sometimes his own feelings. By doing so the relationship between children and teacher can be assumed as companionship. Participation in the debate has to appear to be equal, the teacher as a part of the group.

This group however is a purely artificial assemblage. It is built via the institution. It depends on the institutional frame in emergence and maintenance. And with the institutional frame the institutional rules, regulations, norms, values, beliefs are inseparably conjoined. In mainstream schools equality between teachers and children is always restricted by institutional role definition. It is the teacher who is responsible for what the child does. It is the teacher who supervises the child, not vice versa.

In that regard the staging of circle time in real life gives more evidence of the actual situation in pedagogic institutions than the proposals put forward in conceptual papers or manuals. The material performance of the actors in the scene, children and teachers will always be a momentary enacting of the ambiguity that surrounds the complex of authority, discipline, order at the current historical stage.

And yet the symbolism of circle time is a long way away from the one in the line of pairs. Looking at the reality of school practices however we find that in mainstream schools there is a peculiar situation whereby circle time appears alongside the line of pairs. This observation indicates that there must be an ambiguous situation within the pedagogical institution in which the two rituals are staged.

Let us look at the context of German mainstream schools which were referred to in the last section as the school type with a more ambiguous ritual culture. An example from a school in my home town:

At the front door of the school house a white line is put down on the concrete ground. This line marks the place where the pupils are supposed to wait for the supervising teacher before school starts in the morning and at the end of break time. While waiting to be commanded into the school house, the classes are supposed to line up in pairs. Every class has got its own place to assemble. The teacher on yard duty gives the order to enter the classroom. One after the other the classes are allowed to go.

What I describe in the example is the ideal version. In reality the demanded ritual becomes a more and more dysfunctional performance.

This is a good example for the erosion of forms that are running out of time. Several children do not appear where they are expected to be; the line of pairs has very little in common with the ideal cellular shape which was mentioned earlier; often little groups of children are standing in a casual mixture together and some are squirrelling through the bustling crowd. Obviously the scene does not meet the defined targets any longer. Here the ritualised formation gradually vanishes under a sense of common agreement and in terms of the Berlin ritual studies this can be seen as a change via mimesis.

The teachers whose role it would be to represent the demanded targets are recurring to the disciplinary means given to them by status and position only in exceptional cases. Suspension of the normalizing judgement creates a shift in the possibilities to act.

One reason for teachers' hesitation to enforce the rule is the lack of conviction in the functionality of the ritual. In the teaching process in class they often use different variations of organisation of groups and work-processes (of which circle time is only one, others include individual 'week-plans' and differentiated activity schedules) – and by doing so they know themselves absolutely in the mainstream of innovation in the educational system.

Another reason can be found in the economy of acting. To push the normalizing judgement to a certain extent of efficiency is not as easy any more as it was some decades ago. Historical shifts caused a process to open the school which makes it difficult for the pedagogic staff to hold on to traditional mechanisms of penalising, which are often not in line with modern theory.

"School finds itself under permanent social control with changing expectations and partially contrary demands of powerful social groups and institutions. (…) School as a states regulated institution can not avoid to be compared to other social spheres in its process of modernisation and development. This means in particular the issue of defining its aims in competition to other educational institutions and the question how (…) work-styles are critically assessed and developed" (Bildungskommission NRW 1995, p. 78).

However the mentioned permanent social control is a specific one, which causes different results in different spaces, be it in the safe area of the institution covered by walls, fences and hedges or in the outer world. Discourses of innovation are penetrating the virtual territory of pedagogy while on the other hand the physical territories are still closed zones. Hence a paradoxical situation arises. Within the institution the members of staff can feel in a quite comfortable position, protected. This position offers the opportunity for experiments with new ways of teaching and social roles. If one of the experiments should bring unwanted results, the wall prevents its visibility.

But outside of the institution when the territory is left it appears again: the line of pairs. In the very moment when the children step out of the pedagogic resort and move into the world, they are commanded into the formation. The reign of the line of pairs is the strongest where we find the institutionally bound individuals in the open space of the outer world: on the way to the swimming-pool, coming back from the museum etc. Institutional life for periods of traversing public space is uncovered by walls and in fact totally visible to the eyes of the public. The results of these circumstances are apparent. Institutionally defined positions in the various status groups are cast in a material form in the line of pairs.

This now points to the supervision of the supervisors, which they are wary of. Public space is no longer safe territory. "Problems in relation to the supervising duties are regularly emerging in two ways: first as an idea of supervision in the own mind, the fear of … [accusation of] ... not fulfilling supervision duties, [second] the reasonable fear of endangering the entrusted children and youths. The idea of supervision in the own mind is often extensively infiltrated by surreal directions and prescriptions of the administration, which have but few in common with the pedagogic task (...), yet a lot with the intention to cover the institution and its boards perfectly against any possible claim for indemnification and compensation" (F.I.P.P. 1982, p. 15).[22]

The context of control in which the (imagined) observation of the supervisors is located diffusely in the public sphere is not personalised. It mirrors the vanishing of the seeing/being seen-dyad in Bentham's ideal

22 It is common practice for staff in pedagogical institutions to draw a picture of the seemingly 'child-hating administration fuzzies' and thereby assuming oneself on a higher pedestal of child-friendly morale. In a wider context this assumed contradiction is nothing than two sides of the same coin. Pedagogy is always bound to institutional context and thus undividable of administrational interests. Both are corresponding in a cooperative tension.

panoptical space. The permanent expectation to be seen causes the permanent control of behaviour.

Led through the hostile world, the children are ordered to obey the rules of ceremonial representation of the constitutive difference of status in the institution. So the anxiety on the side of the adults in charge about denunciations out of the suspected observation by 'third parties' is calmed down. You never know who's passing by: no experiments.

Nevertheless what we see in this little excursion is that within schools there is a dynamic at work that leads to changes in ritual cultures over time. In the example of the school with the white line the erosion of the disciplinary form is obvious. At the same time this process is not based on a consciously made decision amongst teachers to abandon the practice. If that was the case the white line would be gone, or simply ignored completely. It is not. Hence the teachers (and children) act out the ambiguity that is characteristic for the wider pedagogic discourse in which the school is embedded.

For teachers being actors in this dynamic the question arises, how much of their acting is actually anchored in an effort to take ownership of their own actions, individually and even more important as a collective. To gain agency of one's own action a consciousness of these actions is necessary. For teachers to reflect on the rituals they enact in their professional practice then seems to be a must.

Chapter 4 Interlude: Reflection

4.1. Introduction

For a teacher to state publicly that she or he does not reflect on their practice is anathema. The proliferation of the catchy slogan of the teacher as reflective practitioner clearly has a prescriptive character: it formulates a demand as much as an obligation.

In section 1.7. an overview was presented on the suggestions made by various authors who wrote on rituals in school in relation to the complex of reflection on those rituals. The close link between rituals and belief systems, the dominantly analogic form of communication in rituals, their character as unquestionable practices where mentioned as elements that would make reflection difficult. Michael Göhlich is the only author who stated explicitly that the cultural and historical background, the underlying power relations, and the fact that rituals can actually be changed, all can be uncovered by conscious efforts (Göhlich 2004, p. 22). With a view on the practice of teachers then the question arises: Do teachers reflect on rituals in school? Furthermore if ritualisation is seen as situational strategic intervention in negotiations of power relations a particular interest arises in the interactive reflection processes of teachers. Thus also: Can the process of reflection be described? Can typical patterns be identified in the professional reflection processes of teachers in primary schools concerning rituals/ritualisations?

In a way similar to the uncertainty that surrounds the term ritual it is quite obvious that there are also a significant number of attempts to present concepts of reflection. It seems inevitable that with the growing popularity of a term (not only) within educational scientific discourse the number of its interpretations and uses grows accordingly. Before turning to concrete reflection processes on rituals therefore it makes sense to sketch some ideas on reflection. I will do so by referring to three models of classification. They depict reflection according to processual scale, functional character or orientational character.

4.2. Processual Scale of Reflection

Morwenna Griffiths and Sarah Tann present a theory of different levels of reflection of which they also note that "not only does it recognise different levels (and purposes) but also asserts that *all* of them are both necessary and important" at different stages in the life of a professional:

1. Rapid reaction;
2. Repair;
3. Review;
4. Research;
5. Retheorising and Reformulating.

On the first level (rapid reaction) one reacts immediately. There is no further process of engagement of thought as a mediation between action and reaction, one can say the action triggers an immediate response. On the second level the reaction as triggered by the initial action is delayed and a process of 'on-the-spot' and very quick thought leads to a reworked plan that is similarly 'on-the-spot' enacted. Griffiths/Tann note on the fleeting nature of this process that "an untrained observer will miss it" (Griffiths/Tann 1992, p. 78).

Reflection processes on the third level take place after the situation has lapsed. The situation will have left a lasting impression and it is this impression that is observed. As teacher educators Griffiths/Tann refer to examples, e.g.: "A teacher may reassess how a child is to be managed, or think again about group relations in the class" (Griffiths/Tann 1992, p. 78). Such thought may happen at various times and in various contexts, break time, in staff rooms before or after school, in the car on the way home.

The next level of reflection includes a systematic observation that will provide the material for the reflection. Collecting such material can take significant periods of time, Griffiths/Tann mention weeks or months. Once sufficient material is together, "the teacher will then reflect carefully on the reasons for the way the issue has arisen in the way it has, and also on the information collecting itself: its validity and reliability" (Griffiths/Tann 1992, p. 79).

Eventually on the fifth level personal theories that guide practice are revealed and scrutinized, challenged, compared to public theories, and consequently confirmed or reconstructed in the process of reflection. But similarly the public theories will be critically examined and assessed for their validity.

4.3. Functional Character of Reflection

In his monograph on transformational learning Jack Mezirow (1991) presents a scheme in which he differentiates reflection according to its function into content reflection, process reflection and premise reflection.

One's feelings, perceptions, thoughts or actions provide the material for reflection. In content reflection these are taken up as given, the guiding question is: what is it, that I feel, see, think or do. These observations are used then to judge, assess a certain situation and consequently act according to this judgement.

In process reflection the focus shifts on the process of problem solving. The question is how the functions of feeling, perceiving, thinking or acting are performed and in consequence on the assessment of how efficient they are performed.

In premise reflection eventually the question is asked why we feel, perceive, think or act in the way we do. This leads to an “assessment of the validity of norms, roles, codes, 'common sense’, ideologies, language games, paradigms, philosophies, or theories that we have taken for granted” (Mezirow 1991, p. 105). Thus premise reflection is less concerned with problem solving than it is with problem posing. This includes making the familiar a problem, putting up for scrutiny what seems most natural, raising questions about the validity of taken-for-granted assumptions.

One of the main references on which Jack Mezirow builds his model of reflection is Jürgen Habermas. From him Mezirow draws the notion of three broad areas in which knowledge is produced: the technical, the practical and the emancipatory (Habermas 1968). The technical is representative of the domain of instrumental learning. The practical represents the domain of communicative learning. Knowledge generated on basis of emancipatory interest eventually "involves a learning dimension of critical reflection with implications for both of the other two" (Mezirow 1991, p. 73). It is obvious how the concept of content, process and premise reflection mirrors this schema.

4.4. Critical Reflection – Orientational Character of Reflection

In Jack Mezirow's concept, the notion of critical reflection is already contained. Probably the most prolific protagonist of critical reflection is Stephen Brookfield. For Brookfield the general process of reflection involves the four stages: identifying assumptions, validating of assumptions, changing perspective, taking informed action. As such these four stages (hence: reflection) can be applied in each and any process of thinking about a situation that is experienced as problematic. Brookfield sees them as the "technical aspects of reflection" (2010, p. 218).

Reflection is not critical per se. It is possible to reflect on "the nuts and bolts of classroom processes" only. "For example, we can reflect about the timing of coffee breaks (...) or how rigidly we stick to a deadline for the submission of students' assignments. All these decisions rest on assumptions that can be identified and questioned, and all of them can be looked at from different perspectives. But these are not, in and of themselves, examples of *critical* reflection" (Brookfield 1995, p. 8).

For Brookfield to speak of 'critical reflection' implies a transformational difference to speaking of 'reflection' because of the idea of criticality being grounded in critical theory. Reflection thus can not be construed as critical if it focuses on increasing efficiency or productivity within an existing system. It necessarily has to call into question the foundations and imperatives of the system (Brookfield 2010, p. 219). In his own view what makes reflection critical is the purpose of externalizing and investigating power relations, and of uncovering hegemonic assumptions. Thus ideology critique is one of the central features of critical reflection. Brookfield holds that within the framework of critical reflection "teaching practices, professional and ethical codes, and accepted modes of decision-making [are] contested – phenomena containing the contradictory crosscurrents of the struggle for material superiority and ideological legitimacy that exist in the world outside" (Brookfield 2010, p. 222).

Essential for an understanding of critical reflection as suggested by Brookfield is that the actual subject matter to be reflected upon is seen as social practice in which power relations are always already at work. In this way Brookfield's theory also relates to what Michel Foucault depicts as "a certain way of thinking, speaking and acting, a certain relationship to what exists, to what one knows, to what one does, a relationship to society, to culture and also a relationship to others that we could call, let's say, the critical attitude" (Foucault 1997, p. 42). For Foucault a critical attitude raises the perpetual question: "How not to be governed *like that,* by that, in the name of those principles, with such and such objectives in mind and by means of such procedures, not like that, not for that, not by them" (Foucault 1997, p. 44).

Critique then is "the art of voluntary insubordination, that of reflected intractability," it problematises the subjugation of individuals in "the reality of social practice through mechanisms of power that adhere to a truth" (Foucault 1997, p. 47). Turned back onto the idea of critical reflection we see how a reflection process that aims on externalizing and investigating power relations or uncovering hegemonic assumptions relies on the critical attitude as an underlying orientation. In this sense we can understand the classification of a reflection process as "critical" as a description of the orientational character of the reflection.

4.5. The Importance of Reflecting with Others

The lack of input of others in reflective processes in solitude is a limitation. Only in communication with others the own thoughts become more objectively visible to oneself, take definable shape and are made open to revision and refinement (Rodgers 2010, p. 48). This common sense argument is reflected in numerous initiatives as nurtured by school authorities or providers of continuing professional development. "Of course, the concept of doing things together certainly is not new. The educational landscape is littered with an alphabet soup of collaborative initiatives – NLCs (networked learning communities), PLCs (professional learning communities), IKCs (innovative knowledge communities), COPs (communities of practice), etc. " (Katz/Dack/Earl 2009, p. 36).

Neville Hatton and David Smith (1995) in their much cited article on reflection in teacher education draw on the importance of having others as partners to facilitate reflection as reported by student teachers. In interviews on their experiences with reflection the student teachers identified particularly two strategies as helpful, both of which included a "high degree of verbal interaction with trusted others" (Hatton/Smith 1995, p. 41). "Critical friend" dyads and staff supervised peer group discussions were reported as overwhelmingly effective in facilitating reflection.

It does not need any further explanation that a change of perspective rests on the availability of another perspective and that obviously the exchange, communication, discussion with others provides the opportunity to obtain such a different perspective. Xiaodong Lin and Daniel Schwartz have made the point that even where reflection takes the form of an internal dialogue within the mind of one person it still is to be seen as social, a view which they find supported by Piaget: "Reflection is nothing other than internal deliberations, that is to say, a discussion which is conducted with oneself just as it might be conducted with real interlocutors or opponents. One could say then that reflection is internalized social discussion (just as thought itself presupposes internalized language)" (Piaget 1967; quoted in: Lin/Schwartz 2003, p. 10).

The social character of reflection is also highlighted by Alan Ovens and Richard Tinning (2009) who pay specific attention to reflection as situated practice. In their study they explore how student teachers enact reflection differently in different settings. It is no surprise that they find that the "discoursive context the individual is situated with" (p. 1130) has a strong influence on the reflection processes that these students report.

As for teachers it is however not at all clear what exactly happens in situations in which they are reflecting on rituals in school. Communication is not necessarily the same as reflection, and as we have seen already, there are a number of different ways to look at reflection. The particular emphasis laid on the social aspect of reflection is well summed up in the context of the idea of critical reflection by Stephen Brookfield who suggests that "critical reflection is an irreducibly social process" (Brookfield 1995, p. 141). He points to the value of colleagues' perceptions in gaining a clearer perspective on one's practice, but also to the importance to realise that individual experiences that appear to be problematic are in fact shared by others, too.

And he warns that conversation as such is not necessarily critical. "Indeed, teacher talk can easily become a swapping of mutually reinforcing prejudices, an experience in group think. (...) Putting teachers together in a room and suggesting that they talk about what they do will not necessarily increase the amount of critical reflection in the world" (Brookfield 1995, p. 142).

Chapter 5 Reflecting on Rituals: Negotiating Legitimacy

5.1. Introduction

The various attempts to conceptualise reflection offer a spectrum of possibilities to describe reflection processes. Models of processual scale (Griffiths/Tann), functional character (Mezirow), and orientational character (Brookfield) can be helpful in doing so. There are however also limitations in these concepts. If we want to understand why *these* teachers in *this* school do or don't reflect on rituals/ritualisations, or do reflect on rituals/ritualisations in this form, to this extent and not in another it seems vital to enhance the figures of thought applied to the concepts of reflection.

Reflection happens in a given situation. It is context-bound within a specific constellation of time/space/environment. In its reference to a subject matter – in this case rituals/ritualisations as concrete acts of concrete actors – reflection is always concerned with the search for a definition of reality.

As such when teachers reflect they negotiate different options of defining the concrete acts on which they reflect. Reflection in this sense can not be understood as a neutral activity. While reflection offers ways of understanding it also excludes other ways which in a social context plays a role for the way how reality can be articulated for "cognitive endorsement by all" (Bell 1992, p. 131).

Looking at the environment of school it is clear that we deal here with an organisation in which there are always others. There is no such thing as the lonely teacher who acts free of all bounds. Rituals understood as actions that are expressive, constitutive or modifying of social order, norms, values are public practice even were they happen in a classroom with the door closed. Ritualisations in terms of Catherine Bell's suggestion are similarly social action. They make sense only in the context of a social situation.

Teachers reflecting on rituals with others in their professional practice need to be seen as actors acting in a social situation. In this sense one should think of reflection of teachers in their professional environment as yet another situational strategic activity, here: of defining and articulating reality in negotiation with their partners in the reflection setting. These parameters will be contextualised in the next section where coverage will also be given to examples as derived from the collection of material accumulated in the interview series in the course of my research.

5.2. Ritual Experts Reflecting Amongst Themselves

In the reflection processes that the teachers reported in their interviews a number of themes can be deciphered:

Negotiating harmonised practice

Confirming demarcation lines

Negotiating non-conforming position

Undercover rumblings

Discussing scripts and choreography of ritual

Negotiating ritualisation (formalisation) of activity

Negotiating de-ritualisation (de-formalisation) of activity[23]

Defining teachers role in community

Negotiating ritual leadership

Trading tips and tricks (old – new teachers)

Review practice against conceptual ideas

These rubrics provide keywords for the description of themes that are at play in teacher's reflection processes on rituals. This is not to be seen as a typology of pure categories into which the various examples can be neatly placed. In each process there can be more than one of these themes at play, hence in many cases a given example could be subsumed

23 The terms ritualisation and formalisation are not used as interchangeable here, thus the brackets around 'formalisation'. Formalisation has to be understood as an aspect of ritualisation (see: Bell 1997, pp. 138 – 169).

under more than one theme. This is a consequence of the multi-layered nature of the processes.

At the same time for developing the themes it is necessary to attend to them separately. For this purpose I will present a variety of examples with paraphrased reports of the actual reflection process or direct quotes (*in italics*) from the interviews. The examples are numbered and a heading is added for each for better referencing.

All examples referred to by teachers in mainstream schools, Irish and German, are about reflection processes with colleagues. Parents and pupils don't feature as partners for reflection on rituals. In free alternative schools the majority of reflection processes reported in the interviews is also amongst colleagues, while there are examples also of reflection processes together with pupils.

As a distinction in this regard I wish to come back to Catherine Bell's notion of ritual specialists or ritual experts (Bell 1992, pp. 130 – 140). The authority of teachers derives from their position as office holders within the educational system. They are members of the corps of staff who are collectively representing this system and are responsible for the upholding of its ethos. In shaping their everyday practice they exercise the "formulation of reality" (Bell 1992, p. 131).

Where teachers reflect upon rituals with colleagues this can be seen as negotiation of practice amongst ritual experts, and as we will see exactly this is what happens in the vast majority of all cases that teachers in the interviews report about. All examples refer to practices in school that the teachers understood to be rituals. It would be possible also to analyse the reported activities for their ritual qualities. This however would lead too far away from the current purpose which is to concentrate on the reflection processes on rituals.

5.2.1. Negotiating Harmonised Practice

In mainstream schools teachers find themselves in a situation where they are individually responsible for what happens in the classroom. However they are not free to do whatever they like. The formal boundaries are set by education law. But more important on an everyday level their practice in the classroom is also measured against the practice in the parallel classrooms and the entire school.

In mainstream schools there will always be a field of tension in which the autonomy of a teacher to structure the classroom-life is contrasted to the demand for a school-wide coherence in terms of practices. This is even more obvious in those spaces that are deemed to be common spaces: corridors, assembly-halls, libraries, school-yard etc. A lot of time can be spent in a school environment to negotiate harmonised practice in a bid to increase the consistency of practices throughout a school.

In free alternative schools the demarcation line of the classroom door is hardly ever present in the same way as in mainstream schools. In most of these schools there are also at least two, often three or four adults working together in taking care of a group of children. The concrete presence and practice in shared spaces triggers discussions about consistency even faster.

As a theme the negotiation of harmonised practice is part of many reflection processes on rituals. The following examples are taken from interviews with German mainstream teachers. However the theme is just as much present in examples that are listed further below, e. g. in the rubrics of non-conforming, demarcation lines or de-ritualisation.

1 Seating Order

In a German mainstream school three teachers in parallel classes have an agreement that the seating order of the children in class is shuffled regularly by the teacher. This is harmonised between the section team members. The teacher has a monopoly on putting children into a seating order. She shuffles this order every 4 weeks in a little ritual (having cards with names, putting them to tables …).

After a parents meeting where the practice is questioned by some parents the topic is brought up in a sectional staff meeting. In reviewing their practice, they try to analyse how it works in the various classes and how the teachers cope with certain elements of the process (e. g. Is the time of shuffling as loud in your class as in mine?). It is also put up for discussion whether the principle of teachers monopoly should be maintained as strict, or should exceptions be allowed for children who absolutely don't get on with each other.

Teacher 'A' leads the discussion with her arguments, being aware of the critical aspects of exercising adult authority, but using it to establish (democratic) values in class: tolerance, equality, respect, inclusiveness – in countering cliques and bitchiness. Teachers 'B' and 'C' are d'accord with this view. The general decision to have the practice in the parallel classes is confirmed in the process.

Comment

The teacher who reported the example stated that she and her colleagues have a similar basic orientation towards teaching. They share a set of values that often collide with the formal demands laid on them by the mainstream school system. On basis of their shared orientation they find it easy to reflect upon issues like the seating order. They measure their practice against their own orientation, and try to find a way how to bring their values to bear in the concrete classroom situations. For them harmonising practice amongst their parallel classes is also a means to win a stronger position vis-à-vis parents or colleagues. Their reflection process as described here can be read as a re-affirmation of their practice, a check if there is a need to re-negotiate their harmonised practice. The reflection takes place in a sectional staff meeting. These meetings are held on a weekly basis which provides the opportunity to come back to a given topic without too much time delay on a regular basis.

2 Establishing Ritual Charter

A new principal starts in a German mainstream school. She realises that there are quite different practices in the various classrooms. She suggests a staff planning day on rituals with the aim to harmonise practice. Three subgroups are working on topics: class representatives; reading time; morning circle.

In the working group on morning circle there are six teachers. They tell each other about their own practice 'how to morning-circle'. There is general consensus amongst the teachers that *"it is good as a ritual"* particularly in the form of a circle because *"all children get their share, it has to do with them personally, not with subject matter, but rather with their everyday life."* What differs are the exact details of activities. One teacher proposes story-writing, another one singing, a third one story-telling. The differences are noted and pros and cons are discussed.

The working group puts together a suggestion for the plenum in which building blocks for a harmonised morning-circle are presented. In the plenum the working group explains the suggested building blocks with some examples. The plenum agrees to the suggested concept as a framework for all classes.

Three elements are made binding: the circle as a shape (formation); a how-are-you round; visualisation of daily planner. The implementation is followed up by the principal, checking on teachers.

There is no repeated reflection or review however on staff level within two years. The concrete practices of teachers are yet different. On everyday level during the school year no reflection happens on this issue. The classroom door is still a demarcation line. It is only for the principal to cross it.

Comment

The staff planning day dealing with rituals in school explicitly addresses the question of harmonised practice. It is initiated by the principal who finds that there is not enough school-wide consistency in the various classes.

In the actual discussion in the working group the focus lies on technical aspects of 'how to morning-circle'. The discussion amongst teachers then brings a result best described as minimal agreement. It is a compromise that is bearable for all teachers. It does not cut too deep into their individual autonomy as territorial authority within the classroom situation. The demand of the principal for a harmonisation is met, but at the same time the harmonisation is warded off to a great degree. As the teacher in the interview observes the concrete practice from class to class differs.

3 Holding Back Strategically

A 55 year old teacher 'D' starts a job at a new German mainstream school. She has been formerly vice-principal in another school and has worked in teacher education also. There are 13 members of staff in the school.

After half a year a colleague 'E' requests in a staff meeting that *"rules are obeyed"* and children are lined up after break time. With her request 'E' refers to another colleague 'F' who does not line up children of her class. At this stage 'D' realises that there is a rule at the school for lining up children. She has not done that either with her class. She dislikes lining up as a disciplinarian measurement.

'D' in the staff meeting points to the disciplinarian character of lining children up. Another colleague responds that order and freedom are not necessarily adverse to each other. 'D' in the interview: *"At this point I was aware: ooops, aahm, yes, and it was clear for me, the atmosphere was like, no-one wanted to make this into something big. I could sense this also when I said, 'O.K., I see that there was a resolution made, and sure for the time being I will follow it.' It was like a sigh of relief, the general mood, everyone appeased, yes. And I thought, O.K., I can not start at the school here and immediately try to overthrow these resolutions."*

Consequently she does not push for further discussion.

Comment

On the one hand the teacher who took part in the interview is quite clear in her dismissive position towards lining up. On the other hand she also measures efforts and effects when deciding not to enter into a discussion on the issue with her colleagues. As a new member of staff she feels she needs to be careful not to be isolated. Stephen Brookfield has suggested the term 'cultural suicide' as a possible consequence for teachers bringing up confrontational issues. This is something the teacher in the example tries to avoid.

She is further aware of the effort that it would take to pre-structure the field if she wanted to change the resolution. In the interview she mentions that she would have to talk to colleagues individually first (suss out, make allies, connect, get information for possibly confrontational argument). Her position as an experienced colleague (age, but particularly also: status as a lecturer in teacher education and former vice-principal) in her eyes gives her a certain protection, but it does not make her untouchable. She compares this with her situation when she was vice-principal where she was able to push topics on the agenda or even push for certain results simply because of her status position.

The reflection process about lining up in the staff meeting dies a sudden death. It remains a process of negotiating harmonised practice, here in the form of reprimanding colleagues who don't stay in line. There is a sharpness in this process that is different to discussion about harmonising classroom practices in example 2. Lining up happens in the school-public area, in common spaces, school yard and corridors. It is here where compliance is claimed by other staff. The demarcation line of the classroom door does not protect from this sort of criticism.

5.2.2. Confirming Demarcation Lines

Where rituals in class are concerned teachers can fend off attempts to harmonise practice relatively easy on the basis of their sole responsibility for what's going on behind the classroom door. As long as there is no infringement of legal requirements it is left to the teacher to structure practice. Reflecting on classroom practice thus can easily shift towards the theme of confirming demarcation lines. This can be seen from examples of German mainstream schools:

4 Talk Without Consequences

In the staff meeting in a German mainstream school the 13 teachers exchange examples of their own classroom practices. This is meant as a means to get new ideas. One teacher presents morning circle as a means of social learning. She would like to see others also engage in daily circle time. Others say they don't have time to do morning circle, they have too much *"stuff to cover"* (subject matter, curriculum). Others reckon that morning circle may be a good idea on a weekly basis. The discussion has no consequences. It is left to each teacher to do or not to do morning circle.

Comment

A reflection process like this is a way to confirm demarcation lines simply by not bringing together the strings in discussion. Arguments are put up, but they remain unmediated, standing opposite of each other: social learning vs. curriculum delivery. At the end of the day it is left to each teacher to do whatever they wish with the arguments. No-one will charge at them as long as they keep to their classroom boundaries.

This however is not the full story. For the teacher in this example there is a distinct problem because of the coordination between parallel classes of subject matter to be covered in certain time spans. Dates for written tests are set for all parallel classes for the year in advance. The subject matter to be dealt with in the tests is to be the same for the parallel classes. This puts pressure on the teachers to work through the subject matter with their classes at the same speed. If a class lags behind, the test results will automatically be worse. Her parallel class colleague who is a stalwart of curriculum delivery works away faster with the subject matter, hence she has to follow suit – or at least feels under pressure to do so. In these circumstances daily morning circle can indeed create a time problem.

The discrepant attitudes and the resulting pressure on the teacher who favours circle time as a means of social learning however is not addressed in the reflection process. The demarcation line of the classroom door provides a peculiar protection for the teacher who sets the pace in covering subject matter. Demarcation is in fact adhered to only where it is about certain aspects, here: the idea of social learning. Where it is about the principle of performance and curriculum delivery the classroom doors are not a barrier at all.

5 Tally Sheets and Traffic Lights

In a German mainstream school a teacher teaches two subjects in a class that is not her own. The class teacher in this class has a system of demerits: a child who is 'inattentive' or 'disruptive' gets a tick on a tally sheet. The subject teacher does not like the tally sheet. In her opinion it is *"negative conditioning."*[24] However she uses the system while teaching her subjects.

After a while she finds, it does not work for her. She introduces instead her own system: traffic lights on tables.[25] With this system she is more comfortable. In informal exchange with the class teacher both confirm that for each of them their own system 'works' and thus they both 'leave each other alone'.

"Q – Did you discuss with your colleague that you do that differently? And what sort of discussion was that, what did she say?

A – Well, she basically said the same thing, she said that in her opinion the traffic light system is hard to handle and she doesn't cope well with it, but she said at the same time, if it works for me, then it is O.K. with her if I use it in her class."

This discussion happened at the beginning of the school year. The interview was held at the end of the school year and no further discussion on the topic happened between the two teachers since.

Comment

It is pretty obvious how the two teachers divide the territory amongst themselves. It is worth remembering that this was stated as an example by the teacher in the interview for a reflection process on a ritual. However what is going on in this reflection process is best described as a confirmation of demarcation lines. Exchange about the actual ritual remains on the level of asking: Does it work for you? If yes, stick to it. If no, use your own system. At the end of the day it is you who is responsible for what happens behind the classroom door.

Obviously there is no discrepancy in the principle that underlies the two demerit-systems, the difference is on the level of technical devices used to make the ritual happen. Therefore it is even easier for the two teachers to agree on the demarcation.

---

24 In the language of behaviourist theory this should be "conditioning of negative behaviour."

25 For an account on the 'traffic light system' see appendix.

6 How to Start PE

A teacher 'G' starts her first job after the final exam in a German mainstream school. She teaches PE in different classes. There are two colleagues who also teach PE. The three teachers come together for a sectional staff meeting at the beginning of the school year.

In the meeting the new teacher brings up rituals for starting and finishing a PE-lesson of which she holds they are important *"to mark beginning and end."* One colleague 'H' who also starts new at the school rejects the idea with the argument that it is too time consuming. The other colleague 'I' who is at the school for a long time states that the idea is interesting. In the discussion the different lines of argument are put up but there is no scrutinising of them.

In practice 'G' introduces her ritualised ceremonies. 'H' and 'I' don't pick up on it.

Comment

In this case the teachers in question do not all agree to drawing the demarcation line. In fact 'G' would be quite happy to break it down – on her terms. She also feels that she can win an argument. She is self-confident about her practice, not the least on basis of her teacher training.

"I learned that during my practical year. I had a fantastic lecturer. From her we learned that it makes sense for PE also that the children know: now we start. (...) And that was the first thing that I did with my class in PE and I found that they took to it immediately, that was great, so that I have a ritual at the start and the end in PE."

However when her colleagues don't share her enthusiasm 'G' does not escalate the discussion. *"And because it was at the beginning of the school year (...) I guess I didn't dare to say, to also say vehemently: 'But truly you have to do that for this and that reason.' Instead I accepted that she told me: 'I won't do it. Do you know how much time that would take?' And I said: 'Well, if that is how you look at it.'"* She is also acutely aware of her position as a new teacher. *"And if you are new in the place you don't really dare with a colleague, and I am personally like, ahm, that I thought by myself, hey, slow down. I don't want to stand out here like: look at her, straight from teacher training, has not a clue yet and thinks she could tell me how to teach PE."*

The reflection process on the rituals for starting and finishing PE-lessons consequently remains a process of confirming demarcation lines.

5.2.3. Negotiating Non-conforming Position

As noted earlier rituals bring with them an obligation to participate. "On the side of the institution any uncertainty in the execution is primarily understood as resistance and in certain cases consequently penalised, even where it happened through momentary lack of concentration only" (Hamm 1999, pp. 18/19). To not do ritual while the rest does is legitimately possible only on basis of a verdict that guarantees absolution for such non-conforming.

Negotiations of non-conforming positions are another common theme in reflection processes reported in the interviews.

7 Special Needs Pave a Way Out

In an Irish primary school parents of a child with 'special needs' approach the resource teacher. The child has problems with lining up in the morning before school. The child is afraid of being too close to others with the movement all around.

The resource teachers brings this up in a sectional staff meeting. All teachers agree to observe the child in the morning. They discuss about their observations in the next sectional staff meeting. All teachers share the impression as reported by parents. The teachers agree to advise parents to bring the child a little later and time the arrival at school so that the other children are already gone in (or in the process of doing so).

Comment

What is reported here by the teacher in the interview as a reflection process on lining up is very much a negotiation of a non-conforming position for a child. There is no discussion about the ritual as such, in fact *"it was taken as granted that the children couldn't come in en masse into the building. You know, we knew that. That wasn't up for debate because of the safety of all the children. That couldn't be up for debate."*

The reflection process then is about a) confirming that the child in question is not 'malevolently' playing up, that there is a 'deficit' that b) allows for absolution to be granted for non-conforming.

8 Messing Up the Line

In a German mainstream school the (unwritten) rule is that classes line up after yard break. One teacher (not the one participating in the interview) reports in the staff meeting that with her class this does not work – the children are constantly fighting in the line.

In the ensuing discussion some teachers, depicted in this case as the *"older colleagues,"* are of the opinion that children should be able to line up and it should in fact be required that they do it. Their argument is *"it should not be a problem to line up in pairs behind each other. That was done in kindergarten already and now they are in school. And the children need to learn the rules, and if we don't teach them now, when should they learn it at all?"* However other teachers also confirm that lining up is generally messy. It is consequently interpreted amongst the teachers as a matter of lacking supervision. There are two parts to the yard that are separated by a building and children are lining up in different parts of the yard. To make the lining up more orderly the teachers decide that all children are to line up in the same part of the yard where they are easier supervised by one staff member.

This is tried and it works better, but the teacher with the original problem class brings the topic up in staff meeting again. She reports that it still does not work for her class. There are *"ruffians in this class who push front, back and sideways with whom lining up is simply impossible."* This time an agreement is found amongst staff for this class to be allowed to go to the classroom without lining up.

Comment

That lining up does not work in the particular class is the children's fault. They are constructed as deficit children, ruffians or thugs. On this basis they are granted absolution for not participating in the ritual. The pattern is similar to example 7. The price however is a stigmatisation that is carried over into the children's public opinion, too.

The teacher in the interview: *"Well, my children would have asked me: 'Miss H., there is no teacher with the class yet and they go into the building already.' They basically told me that there was something not right and that the others were not allowed to go in already. Then I explained to my children that we have an exception of the rule because there are always problems with this class."*

The entire reflection process can be depicted as a succession of

a) Negotiation of non-conforming position: request voiced by teacher 'on behalf' of her class;

b) Negotiation of harmonised practice: initial answer to the request;

c) Negotiation of non-conforming position: renewed request, this time granted by staff meeting.

The teacher who took part in the interview is not the teacher whose class was granted exemption from lining up. It would be only speculation to comment any further on the motivation of this teacher to actually negotiate the exemption for her class, although it would be interesting to follow this up closer. At the end of the day it is also an exemption for the teacher to fulfil her obligation as a member of the corps, makes her life easier even if it is via stigmatisation of the children.

9 Diluted Standards Make Non-conforming Easier

In a German mainstream school the majority of classes are supposed by their teachers to line up after break (or before school) and wait for the teacher to pick them up on the yard. Some teachers however allow the children to simply go into the room at end of break without having to line up and wait to be collected.

The teacher who took part in the interview is of the opinion that lining up is not necessary. She takes over a class in the middle of the school year. The former class teacher insisted that the children line up after break. She informally discusses the topic with a parallel class colleague. This colleague confirms her view that lining up is not necessary with the arguments: the children know anyway where to go, and also for the teacher it gives a few extra minutes to be in the classroom already and prepare for the lesson instead of having to pick up the children on the yard.

The teacher abandons lining up for her class, too.

Comment

In this case there is already a dilution of standards prevalent in the school. The ritual of lining up is not consistently adhered to any more. For the teacher who took part in the interview the reflection with her colleague functions as a catalyst. It is not an accident that she approaches this particular colleague. She knows that this colleague does not insist on the class lining up. She can anticipate that this colleague will support her in an attempt to also abandon lining up with her new class.

The reflection then is a process of negotiating support for each other in non-conforming – in a situation where the ritual at hand is already on a decline in this particular school.

10 No Stepping Out of Line

In a German mainstream school it is obligatory for all teachers to do morning-circle. Also obligatory is that at the start of the week one element of morning-circle is that at the end of the circle the children write a story into a copy-book. The teacher in the interview 'J' reports about a colleague 'K' who finds that in her class the story-writing does not work and talks informally about giving it up in her class. 'J' on hearing this is adamant that 'K' has to comply with the agreed practice. In a staff meeting the topic is brought up:

"Q – And 'K' was of the opinion that she does not need that, does not want that?

A – She does not need that. And that is where we said: No.

Q – She has to do it?

A – She has to do it. It is part of our concept. And, well, of course we didn't say: you have to do that. We rather said, we need to work it out for her to see the point in it. I was, at the beginning, like 'no, no way, she has to, no way she doesn't.' And it was brought into a productive discussion then, more like how can we help this colleague so that her children get this wonderful book, too."

The colleague 'K' consequently continues having children writing a story at the beginning of each week after morning-circle.

Comment

The attempt of the colleague 'K' to sheer out of line is answered by the rest of the staff with a clear message: you stick to the line. In a negotiation of non-conforming in this case no absolution is granted. The colleague is constructed as 'deficit', in 'need of help' – by doing this the potential sharpness of the confrontation is reduced.

We also see here how the negotiation of non-confirming is at interplay with negotiation of harmonised practice. In this case the demarcation line of the classroom door is not accepted. Formally 'K' could certainly sheer out of line, insisting on her role as sole responsible authority in the classroom. However the social cost for such a step could be very high, and it is exactly this what is made clear to her in the staff meeting.

11 Ensuring Compliance

In a free alternative school the school concept refers to 'non-directive' education as a foundation for the actual practice in school. Amongst staff a decision was made to also have 'presentations', that is: adults offering certain topics to children (e. g. long division, dia-show on frogs etc.).

The school hosts three sections: pre-school, primary and SEK 1.[26] In pre-school one teacher 'L' stops offering 'presentations'. She argues that the section is understaffed and also that 'presentations' are not in-fitting with the school concept. Another pre-school teacher 'M', who also is the 'official' sectional team-leader, is not happy with this. However she does not bring it up as a topic in the sectional staff meeting.

Instead she talks to a colleague 'N', the 'official team leader' in the primary section. This colleague has a child in pre-school, thus is a parent also. In a combined staff meeting of primary and pre-school 'N' brings up the topic. In this meeting 'N' argues that presentations are a necessary

26 SEK 1 is a term referring to the first cycle of secondary school (classes 7 – 10 or 5 – 10).

element to also make teachers persons, to give them a status as active members in the school, instead of 'de-personalised' observers only. In this she reminds everyone of the discussion amongst staff that led to the decision to include 'presentations' in the everyday practice. She also argues that extra staff has been recently employed countering the argument of under-staffing. The meeting becomes confrontational. In 'N's report from the interview: *"Well that was no longer, it wasn't a discussion any more. Rather it was, the front was clear, and she had to defend herself, because I had attacked her."*

The combined staff meeting does not lead to a conclusion or result. Instead the topic is discussed again in a pre-school sectional meeting afterwards. Here a decision is made (per majority vote) to have presentations.

Comment

This example mirrors the previous one. Reflection here is similarly a process that aims on ensuring compliance. A difference however is that the sharpness of the confrontation is actually brought to the fore. No attempt is made to interpret non-compliance as a consequence of a 'deficit'. At the end of the day the colleague who stopped presentations is 'put in her place' and is told by the majority of her team that she is obliged to conform (which is also: harmonise practice).

From the description of the process it is also obvious that the sectional team leader of the pre-school 'M' followed a particular strategic path. Instead of directly entering into negotiation (reflection) with 'L' in the pre-school sectional staff meeting she chooses to get 'allies' in the primary section first.

This exemplifies what was pointed out in general terms earlier on, that reflection is as much an act in its own right, a social act in which actors strategically intervene.

12 Playing the Professional Card

In an Irish primary school teachers of 6th class are expected to take part in mass in relation to the confirmation of the children. This mass is held outside school hours on a Sunday.

The teacher in the interview does not want to attend this mass. She thinks that it is the job of the parents to prepare children outside of school, and not the job of the teachers. She also feels *"sometimes religion comes too much into schools."* She approaches the principal and discusses the issue with him.

"A - Aahm, to be honest, he didn't really make to many arguments against what I was saying. I basically said to him that, ahm, confirmation is personal choice, it's religion and. Aahm, I know obviously we do have to teach religion within the school, but I didn't feel that I have to be there for a ceremony that really was the parents responsibility if they wanted their child to take part in it. It's their responsibility and not mine ultimately. I think sometimes religion comes too much into schools.

Q - And did you say that to your principal?

A - Oh, i didn't say that religion comes too much in, but I did say to him that I think we are expected to prepare the children for confirmation whereas their parents, a lot of their parents, I wouldn't say all their parents, quite a lot of the parents have no interest. (...)

This was, this was something maybe, like it's different for say the day of the confirmation where obviously we would, we very much have a huge part in preparing the children for the actual ceremony itself. And that is no problem, you know being at, attending for this one. But Sunday mass it's, it's outside of the school time as far as I'm concerned and at the end of the day I think it's the parents' responsibility. And he was O.K. with that. (...)

You know, he said to me, at the end of the day it's your own choice whether you're there or not. He said, you don't have to be there. He said, Sister X would like you to be there."

Comment

She positions herself as the professional teacher who finishes work on Friday and starts again on Monday. The principal accepts this position, although he points out that 'Sister X', the nun who represents the patron, would like to see the teachers there. This 'negotiation' is one whereby the teacher plays the 'professional' card against the 'religion' card – knowing that she will win this one.

What makes this example specifically interesting is that it is one of only two examples from the entire series of interviews where Irish teachers actually refer to reflection on religious rituals, despite the fact that all of them were quite clear that the term ritual fits best for religious activities.

It is also indicative that the teacher feels a need to negotiate absolution for her non-conforming with the principal although there is by no means a way to reprimand her for not attending a mass outside of school hours. Her approaching the principal then is also an attempt to appease in advance, again: take the sharpness out of a possible confrontation. This is all the more clear when the way how she argues is taken into account: She non-conforms outside of school on the basis of conforming inside of school.

5.2.4. Undercover Rumblings

The second example that relates to religion is from an Irish primary school where the teacher reports of informal exchanges amongst staff. These informal exchanges are also understood to be reflection by the teacher. In her answer on the question whether she has reflection with colleagues outside of formal meetings she says quite typically:

"A - So, we do it, I suppose very informally on a daily basis.

Q - And when do you find time to do that on a daily basis?

A - Aahm, sometimes at the end of the day, break time, after school, you know, I mean, it depends, maybe sometimes during a lesson while the children are working you might have a chance to talk with the teacher to discuss, O.K., what will we do with this child or how will I go about approaching this with somebody. We would do that very informally a lot. (...) you're talking very quickly, maybe, and sometimes it happens, actually it happens a lot before school. A lot of us would be in the school quite early."

It is in these contexts that religious rituals can come up.

13 Corridor Complaints

Teachers in an Irish primary school discuss amongst themselves on informal level about the work load that religious education, particular preparations for confirmation (6th class) lays on them. However these discussions are held informally only and the topic does not come up in formal meetings.

"A - I mean, the confirmation preparation takes up a huge amount of teaching time. It really does, especially for the last term of school, it's in, it just takes up so much time going over rehearse and practising and, it's a huge amount of work. And, really, it's funny, even some of the older teachers would say, they really think, the confirmation preparation should be taken out of the school. And it should be done separately.

Q - Hmhm, yes.

A - So, yes, no there's quite a lot of us who think that.

Q - That is an interesting thing because on the other hand you say, that would not come up as such in a staff meeting.

A - No, nono, wouldn't, it wouldn't be brought up formally, like that wouldn't be discussed in a formal setting. Aahm, it would generally be quite informally, depending on maybe, I suppose whoever was in sixth that year because obviously you have to attend quite a lot of ceremonies and masses and different things. It's usually it affects the sixth class teachers more than anybody else. So, no, it's never been brought up.

Q - Have you a theory why it's not brought up?

A - Aahm, (...) aahm, I think in our case in our school the nun who deals with our school is (...) I think our principal is afraid to bring these issues up with her. I think there's a little bit of, not fear, well, there's a little bit of fear of saying no to her. There is that. And we would, [laughs] we would be afraid to go to her, you know."

Comment

Reflection here remains under the threshold of official exchange of opinion. It is an indicator for the current state of affairs, here: of this particular school. We will see however later that this state of affairs is in fact a rather widespread phenomenon within Irish primary schools. The influence of the church filters through quite strongly. The entire complex of religion in schools, obviously including religious ritual, is approached by teachers with utmost care, so as to not cross a certain line. Open critique, questioning religious rituals in a formal setting is avoided. Instead there are undercover rumblings in form of corridor complaints, mutual affirmation of points of view that one does not dare saying out loud when confronted with a superior member of staff.

5.2.5. Discussing Scripts and Choreography of Ritual

A large number of examples of reflection processes reported by the teachers in the interviews refers to discussions in which the choreography or the script of a given ritual is negotiated. Subsumed under the terms choreography or script are all those elements of a ritual that lead to a certain appearance of the ritual and that are fixed elements in the progression of those acts that make up the ritual. This can be sequences of movements, positions in space that participants are expected to take up, formulas to be said, songs to be sung, particular reactions prescribed in case of certain occurrences.

14 What is a Good Line?

In an Irish primary school children are supposed to line up at the end of yard break. The school has an enrolment of 550 children. There are 24 teachers working in the school. In the monthly staff meeting a teacher brings up the topic of lining up because there are always children who still run around at the end of break.

The reporting teacher does not recall details of the arguments in the ensuing discussion. However she remembers that most teachers would have agreed that the situation could be improved. In the staff meeting a decision is made to set up an incentive. The teacher on yard duty is supposed to give points for lining up to the various classes. Points are counted over the course of a week and the best line of the week is announced.

Comment

What is negotiated here is a technical fix. The teacher in the interview also states that in her opinion *"we're quite weak as a school probably sitting down and reflecting."* She herself keeps a regular journal as a reflective tool for herself. However for a discussion like the one on lining up this has no consequences. She can't remember getting involved in this discussion. The fact that she does not remember any details of the discussion also indicates that there was certainly no controversy around the topic.

15 Honouring Past-pupils

In an Irish 14-teacher school there is a tradition of past pupil achievement celebrations. During a staff meeting a brainstorming process happens in which teachers throw in ideas what elements could be included in the celebrations.

"A - Aah, the caretaker would be assigned the creating of the stage. And class teachers, they would, we decided that we would write a song. (...) One or two of the girls of the staff, said: 'Wouldn't it be lovely if we had a song?'

Q - In the staff meeting?

A - In the staff meeting. Here is the first verse, and word, and then there was throwing ideas out. All you wanted was just one line, and just, the rest of it was repeated, so just to write three or four verses. So the song was written in less than five minutes. It was verse, verse, you know, it was just thrown out together. And then, aahm, what after that, the song, so then we decided there had to be art. So every teacher took the responsibility for getting some kind of art work, stars of flags or whatever. And then coming together on that date, the classes and singing the songs and waving the flags."

As another element of the ritual the seating order in the assembly hall is discussed. However this discussion is held informally:

"A - It's like what's the noise level like. But again, it's not intensive discussion. It might be between four, five members of staff. You know, it doesn't, aahm :

Q – Informal?

A - Informal. Yes. It's not, if, which might work better, if you think that's going to be a long drawn out affair and the infants might get tired, you might keep them in the U-shaped format because it's easier to keep control, or keep, because they're, the rows aren't as long there and they're kind of bunched in a little better and teacher has a better eye on them. You might, instead of rather being fifteen wide, you might have eight wide, three eights as opposed to fifteen, do you know what I mean."

Comment

The discussion is concerned with technical elements of the proposed ritual. It is what Stephen Brookfield calls reflection on the nuts and bolts. Underlying such a reflection is yet an agreement amongst those involved that the particular ritual is actually not questioned as such.

16 Welcoming New Pupils

In a German mainstream school the teachers who are assigned to next year's first class discuss in a sectional staff meeting how to celebrate the first day of school for then new pupils. In their discussion they talk about the various elements that together make up the script for the celebration. A particular aspect that gets attention in the discussion is the question whether the then second class children are to be involved in the celebration. Questions in this regard concern their potential position in the hall, are they going to sit amongst the parents of the new children or will they be backstage. It is also a matter of discussion if the then second class children will take the new children by the hand and lead them to the classroom. Other aspects discussed are the order of presentations on the day and the type of the presentations (songs, stories).

At the time of the interview the considerations on this topic are still ongoing. It is on the agenda for a number of consecutive sectional staff meetings. It will also be discussed by the teachers of the older classes because their classes are supposed to make presentations on the day, too.

Comment

It was mentioned already that the first day of school is a big event in Germany. Preparations for this event are in most cases meticulous. It is a show-piece for the entire school community. Consequently it is no surprise that the teacher in the interview reports of discussions of quite detailed aspects of the ceremony.

While the scale of the event is bigger, the actual matter discussed is similar to the example of the Irish teachers planning a past-pupil achievements celebration.

17 Chain of Sweets

In a free alternative school the annual celebration for new children on their first day of school is discussed. A committee is built from the whole staff meeting to organise the celebration. In the committee ideas for a choreography are collected, sorted and then put into a script for the celebration. Changes are made if elements *"don't feel right."*

"A – We had, earlier there was a chain of sweets.

Q – [laughs] O.K., so you had a chain of sweets, and now you don't have a chain of sweets any more.

A – No, there is no chain of sweets any more. (...) I can't remember, but there may have been a time where we had both, at any rate we thought it would be nice, I think Susanne brought up the idea, ahm (...) to adorn them with a crown of flowers, so that they are quite visible on the day, too. (...) And this is now the established ritual. Well, the sweets are a bit, well, surely, the children like the sweets, but it is not really what we wish to promote."

Comment

The ritual of celebrating the first day of school is as much part of the school culture of this free alternative school as it is in mainstream schools. In the school there is also a strong emphasis on formalised, symbolic performances. Reflecting on the celebration of the first day of school then is a process in which the members of the planning group scrutinise choreography and script for the day according to the elements to *"feel right"* in the context of the school.

18 Farewell to School Leavers

In a free alternative school a parent suggests to 'mark' the farewell for children who move to secondary school. This is not regularly done, but the teacher of the group that leaves the school agrees that the move is a massive step for the children.

Together the parent and the teacher plan the event, consciously as a transition ritual. They deliberately look for symbolic elements to be included in a choreography for a celebration with the children.

"A - We, it was clear to us that we wanted, if you like, a point of departure, where we were leaving this room in which we were for the last year, and where we also don't go back again, leave it behind us in a way. (...) And we thought about ways how to do that. So, we sat in a circle on the floor, we tidied the room completely before, everyone took their personal stuff that they wanted to keep, ahm, and then, exactly, all children had a candle in front of them and I lit up a big candle in the middle and every child then one after the other lit up the own candle with the one in the middle. And then we had a round where everyone could say what they wanted to leave behind and what they wanted to take with them. (...)

And for the leaving behind, we also, everyone could, if they wanted, throw into a litter bin what they wanted to leave behind.

Q – These are a couple of elements, and they are quite symbolic, the candle, the litter bin, ahm, did you discuss the symbolism beforehand?

A – Well, the litter bin, definitely yes. Like, what is there in terms of negative emotions or associations or energies, that that is left behind, symbolised in the litter bin, ahm, and that one can move on to something new without luggage, if you like.

Q – And in discussing with the mother, or also with the children during morning circle, did you explicitly name this as a symbol?

A – In talking with the mother, yes."

Comment

This is the only example from all interviews in which a teacher actually engages with a parent in reflection on a ritual. Their strong anchoring of the choreography in a system of meaningful symbols is quite obvious from the excerpt. The symbolism to which they adhere is a particular way to define and articulate reality, and by putting it into practice in the ritual: for the cognitive endorsement by all.

It is noteworthy yet that this ritual remains a once-off in the context of the school. In the next year the colleague who is with the older children does not pick up the ritual again. It remains a singular event.

19 Stay Overnight in School

In a free alternative school there is a tradition to have an annual overnight stay for all children and all staff. There is a difficulty to find a date due to several activities coming up at once. Amongst staff there is informal talk to cancel the overnight stay for this year. Parents who hear about the idea of cancelling the activity protest and claim that the overnight stay is an important ritual in the life of the school.

The issue is discussed in the staff meeting. One colleague in particular speaks for cancelling the activity.

"She had always hated it. (...) She finds that everyone who sleeps in the school only suffers. The small ones because they can't sleep, the bigger ones also because they can't sleep, only a little bit later around midnight. The next morning everyone is tired and has to spend a full day in school. There is a smell of chemical cleaning agent that is evaporating from the floor, the house is not soundproof at all, you hear every little step."

However she finds herself in a minority position. The majority of teachers find that it is a matter of organising the activity better. Hence the discussion shifts towards an exchange of thoughts of how to plan the overnight stay in a way that makes it less stressful for everyone. A date is picked where the oldest children are actually on their annual school tour and won't be in school, thus the number of children is already reduced. For the day of the overnight stay a number of physical activities (swimming, playground) are scheduled.

Comment

It is an essential element in this school that there is a rather strict division on everyday level between spheres. The school is conceptually defined as a counter-experience to the familial bonds. In this sense the teachers are afforded a role that goes well beyond the idea of a conveyor of subject matter. The overnight stay (as well as the annual school tour) are programmatic elements of the school life in which this counter-experience materialises in particularly strong manner. This is also part of the ritual character of the activity.

If a teacher questions the overnight stay then a different definition of roles looms in the background.

At the beginning of the staff meeting one teacher tries to develop the theme of de-ritualising, simply abandoning the activity. However her attempt is not successful. The question of cancelling the event is not taken up by the majority of the teachers. It is consequently not further dealt with. Instead the theme of script and choreography becomes dominant in the discussion.

Abandoning the overnight stay would be a move to potentially redefine power relations between parents, students and staff – at least in this particular area of school life. By accepting the parents' intervention and by shifting the discussion towards choreography and script the teachers practically confirm the status quo (ante). This process is also a negotiation amongst staff about their definition of their position (reality) in the system of the school.

20 Too Hot on Stage

In a German mainstream school there is an assembly held every Friday at the end of the school week. The assembly is open for parents and there are always parents present. The assembly is regarded as a chance for children to present to the school community what they did during the week. It becomes a topic for discussion when the oldest girls (4th class) start using the stage to perform dances with a sexual character.

"At the beginning that was all right, but then the dances became more and more like the stuff they watch on television. They actually dressed up specifically for it, those little ten year, nine year old girls with those bustiers (...)

And it grew into a problem when certain girls, somehow it was the third Friday and I think it was in fact two times in a row, they used this song that was a hit over here amongst teenagers, the texts are like 'you are so hot' and 'sit on my lap' and all in German and there is a powerful beat in it. And we sat there and (...) well, I sat there and was stuck for words, there was the mother of this one Muslim girl sitting right behind me (...) and I wondered, what she would make of this petty little spectacle there on stage, and what sort of problems it may create for us. I mean, will this woman actually still talk to us. Yes, I nearly froze on my chair.

And then I also saw my boys, and I have a couple of them who are quite advanced in their development, near puberty. They were completely swept off their feet. And, I mean, surely that are nice feelings, too, but it also had, it triggered that during break time then they always followed these girls and didn't leave them alone and I know exactly why, they were hyped up by these half-naked girls."

Members of staff informally (at break time) discuss the girls' performance. Many of the staff members find the performance provocative. The principal brings up the topic in staff meeting.

The teacher in the interview reports that nobody in the staff meeting suggested to simply ban the dances. There is a consensus amongst the teachers that the stage is a deliberately chosen conceptual element in assembly (assembly is seen as ritual) for children to excel on their talents and become self-confident.

On the other hand there is similarly unanimous agreement that the girls' sexualised dance performance presents a problem particularly in relation to families with a Muslim background who account for nearly 70 % of the school population.

In the discussion staff decides to introduce a secretary post for registration of performances for the assembly. The secretary is a teacher (or the principal). If children wish to register a dance, it is checked, whether the dance has been cleared for the stage by the class teacher. Responsibility is thus handed to the individual teachers to allow or not allow a dance to go forward. Teachers in classes then work out with the children such performances that are not regarded as provocative.

Comment

The teachers in this school find themselves in a situation where the children put up questions to them in a sheer practical manner. Weekly assembly is a very important ritual element in this school and its character as a stage for the school community to display itself is clearly wanted by the teachers.

In their discussion in the staff meeting they work out the various lines of argument. Once these lines are clear a practical solution is negotiated amongst teachers. The teachers in fact see themselves in a position where they have to act, they can not not act on the matter because they assume it would have the potential to create massive problems with parents for them. Consequently the preferred solution is one that keeps the sexual energy of the children in check, at least to a point where it is not put on stage.

For this purpose the script for the assembly is changed and a censor is introduced. In this manner it is ensured that the school community in displaying itself keeps to a format that is considered sound and safe by the teachers.

5.2.6. Negotiating Ritualisation (Formalisation) of Activity

Basic to all processes of reflection is that a situation incites perplexity, hesitation, doubt (Dewey 2007, p. 9). Obviously there is an abundance of situations in schools that bear such potential. To find a strategy for dealing with a problematic situation involves reflection. Formalisation and ritualisation of an activity can be one of the problem solving strategies chosen by teachers.

21 Introducing Circle Time

In an Irish five teacher school the topic of anti-bullying-strategies is informally discussed amongst teachers during lunch break. One teacher suggests to try using circle time as a way to address cases of children not getting on with each other. The colleagues agree to try it and after a number of weeks feedback that it works well for them. They also decide to introduce circle time as a standard procedure at the beginning of the year in each class. In this circle time a chart of rules is to be drawn up that is then put up on the wall in the classroom for everyone to see at all times.

This process dates back five years from the date of the interview. Since then no further review or reflection on circle time happened. At the time of the interview it is what the teacher calls *"established practice."*

Comment

Looking at the actual reflection process there are two steps observable. The first one is where the teachers reflect upon anti-bullying-strategies, hence their topic is: Bullying and what to do about it. Circle time comes up as a possible solution. It is tried and after a while a second step happens. Here now a review of the trial phase takes place. The solution is found to be satisfactory. It is consequently agreed as common practice in all classes, although it is not put into the form of a written document or a policy. In due course the practice becomes *"established practice"* and is identifiable as a ritual (or routine).

22 Formalising Dismissal

In an Irish two teacher school the teachers realise that there is a lot of pushing and shoving going on amongst children at the end of the school day when they try to get on the school bus. The teachers informally discuss the issue and agree to organise dismissal in turns, the junior classes first, the senior classes second.

There is no controversy amongst the teachers about the appropriateness of the formalisation of dismissal. They immediately agree that this is a strategy that will solve the problem.

The teacher who took part in the interview teaches the senior classes. She further formalises the process in her class so that 6th class children go first from her room, followed by 5th, then 4th and lastly 3rd class children. She also changes to use the Irish language when releasing the groups. She clearly identifies this practice as ritualistic. Her own choreography is not reflected upon with her colleague.

Comment

The reflection process in this case is a very short affair. There are only two teachers involved, the solution for them seems evident and simple. All that is required to make the formalisation of dismissal workable is a quick agreement whose group is going first.

Such a fleeting and momentary agreement can become a standing ritualised practice quite easily. The same teacher explains how the practice of lining up children was established between her and her colleague. They two work together since 1985.

"A - No, it just seems to happen as such (...) It's sort of, at this stage I suppose we're doing it so long. Perhaps, you know, the first trip we might have gone and we might have said, right, well, you know, we'll put them in pairs, you go the front, I go to the back.

Q - In 1985. [laughs]

A - [laughs] Yes, exactly. At this stage now, you know [laughs], I have to say there's no need for reflection or discussion at it. It happens. It's a ritual [laughs] for the want of a better word."

23 Planning a Ritual Charter

In a German mainstream school a teacher and a trainee teacher who will teach a first class in the following school year come together informally during summer holidays and discuss what rituals they are going to implement. They specifically and consciously discuss this as class rituals.

In their discussion they have as common starting points:

- children need regularity,

- rituals provide regularity,

- rituals are important.

On this basis they plan a number of rituals which they introduce then in their class.

Examples: weekly changing table-chief (a post of responsibility for a child, mainly to fulfil tasks in support of the teacher, e. g. collecting work-sheets or conveying information to the other children); morning-circle (storytelling-time); sound-bowl as means of communication; allocating classroom tasks like watering flowers, sort shoes in shoe-rack, tidy drinking table (the teacher explicitly states that the ritual is not the fulfilling of the task but the allocation of the task, there is a certain time set apart for this in their weekly class schedule).

Comment

There is no controversy amongst the teachers about the appropriateness of the rituals as such. They start from the same platform, having negotiated a common understanding of the meaning of rituals in the context of school (and underlying common ideas about the nature of children or the role of school). The questions they deal with are more on the level of: Which activity shall we ritualise and what choreography shall we give certain rituals, e. g. when allocating tasks having names pulled out of a hat or let children come forward for the various tasks?

5.2.7. Negotiating De-ritualisation (De-formalisation) of Activity

Just as much as ritualisation can be a means for teachers to address a certain situation that appears problematic it is also possible that a ritualised activity can become problematic for teachers in a way that they would rather not have it any more. In the passages on the themes of harmonisation, non-conforming and undercover rumblings examples were already included in which the potential for a negotiation of de-ritualisation was present.

The teacher who holds back in the staff meeting where lining up is discussed strategically decides that it is not the right time and the right place to press ahead. The negotiation about giving up the presentation between the teachers in the free alternative school is shifted towards discussing the non-compliance of the stray colleague, but we remember that this is a result also of the strategic moves of the sectional team leader who secures her allies before directly tackling the issue.

There are however situations in schools also, where teachers see an opening for initiating negotiations with the aim to abandon a particular ritual practice.

24 No More Dictation

A teacher in a German mainstream school attends courses on brain research in relation to learning. The material presented in the courses confirms her opinion that there is no reason to have children write dictation tests.

She reports about the courses in a sectional staff meeting and suggests to abandon the practice of dictation tests in the parallel classes. *"I had a good footing there, I brought all this know-how and then in the sectional meeting I voiced my desire for change: 'I am sure now, I would have done it for a long time, but now there is nothing to stop me. I won't have dictation tests any more. One every semester, that's it.' And they said: 'Wonderful, we join you.'"*

Comment

With her two colleagues the teacher has a very good working relationship. In the interview she describes this situation as one in which mutual respect provides a sound basis for open communication. *"We take each other serious, completely. We respect each other and we critically review our practice, without hurting each other."* They share common views on education. Consequently it is easy for the teacher to bring up the idea of abandoning dictation tests.

Noteworthy also: the tests are not completely abandoned. This points to the wider environment. The school is a mainstream school. She teaches fourth class. Education law requires that there are written tests administered, six per year plus three learning controls. They are to be marked and the marks added up to a half-year and a end-of-year grade. This for her is non-negotiable. She can try to minimise the adverse effects of marking and grading by applying modest standards but she is still obliged to do it. Due to the fact that dictation tests are a common practice throughout most schools there is also pressure on her to show that she has at least covered this area of the curriculum. Hence the moderating *"one every semester."*

In the context of the particular school this however is already a rather radical move. She also reports about earlier years in which there was a different colleague in the parallel class. A reflection process about de-ritualisation in relation to dictation tests would have been impossible.

"That was impossible with my former colleague. We had no way to talk to each other. (...) She was stuck in doing everything as she had done it all the time, and she administered a dictation test every three weeks. I simply had no choice but also have a dictation test every three weeks, although I did not want it."

Objectively it is obviously not true that she had no choice. She could have played out the demarcation line of the classroom door and would have been formally untouchable. But it is also true that she felt that this was not an option that would have promised success. In calculating her strategic position she felt it was the better way not to escalate conflict, particularly also because she did not expect any support for her position from the principal.

With her present colleagues however she feels that there is an opening. Reflection then is easy, they work on common grounds, agreement is reached fast.

25 More No More Dictation

The three teachers who have decided that in their parallel classes dictation tests are reduced to one per semester informally discuss the issue also with other members of staff. This is corridor talk or discussion during yard break.

In their sectional team meeting they decide to also invite an external expert for a staff planning day on the topic. While there is no objection from the principal it still does not happen because of a clash of dates that has the expert unavailable for the day.

Some of the colleagues from other classes then go to attend a lecture of the expert outside school hours. Their feedback afterwards is that they find the expert stupid.

"A – And they came back and said: 'She is stupid.'

Q – O.K., they came back from the lecture with this expert and said: 'She is stupid.'

A – Yes [laughs].

Q – O.K. [laughs] and was that the reflection process then, or what?

A – Well, so far, yes. So far, yes. That is were it is left for now, yes. It has to continue somehow, but for the moment that is it."

Comment

The first step that was made in the sectional staff meeting encourages the teachers to also reach further. Their strategy to go about this business is to first try to secure allies via informal discussion and eventually push for a staff planning day on the matter. Obviously the three teachers feel that it is necessary to engage the colleagues in a discussion that starts on a different level then where they started themselves. The idea to get an external expert in to do a seminar on the topic is in fact a didactic approach. The three teachers intend to teach their colleagues, but they are aware of the difficulty resulting from their status as peers. The expert seems the better solution.

With some of the colleagues coming back from the external lecture with this expert and dismissing her as stupid an impasse looms.

This is the situation at the time of the interview.

It is also worthwhile to highlight the importance of the temporal fit in the interplay of events. The courses attended by the teacher who brought up de-ritualisation in the first instance provide a sound basis for argumentation to make her point. As a reflection setting that is separate in space and time from the actual school in which the teacher works these courses are a chance to take a step back from the actual daily struggles. However the information from the courses can be transferred into the concrete school situation only on the basis that the teacher feels it safe to do so. With the old colleague gone and the two new colleagues at her side the teacher now sees a historical opening.

26 Harmonisation Obsolete

In a free alternative school a teacher is on maternity leave. She will take up her position again after the summer holidays. On some days before the holidays she 'sits-in' to get accustomed to the group that she will work with. She observes morning circle and finds it dysfunctional. Children are not interested, are bored, sit through or disturb.

She discusses her observation with the two colleagues who are in the group. She offers arguments for analysing the situation: children don't need daily morning circle. She also uses the school concept as a point of reference.

"It is necessary to understand how our school works, yes, it's a case that if we are offering something the children are invited to take part. Thus I assume that if I am together with a group, that this group is made up of children who actually want to participate."

In the observed situation however she finds that children do not want to participate, hence she suggests to abandon the daily morning circle.

While her colleagues share the impression that children are bored and often disturb the morning-circle, they yet analyse the situation differently. In their opinion it is a matter of structuring the morning-circle differently.

After the summer holidays the situation changes radically because the colleagues leave the school to work in another job. She takes over the group and scraps the daily morning circle.

Comment

In the free alternative school the reflection process is amongst staff who are supposed to work together as a team in the same room with the same children. There is no way for them to draw a spatial demarcation line similar to the classroom door. Their discussion touches on the compatibility of the ritual with the conceptual orientation of the school. In practical terms the three teachers would have to find a common position to be able to work together after the summer holidays. Their different interpretations and analysis of the situation indicates that there could easily be a problem for them to come to a result in their discussions that is satisfactory for everyone. There is pressure however on them to achieve such a result. When working together with the same children in the same rooms harmonisation of practice is a must, at least to the point where constant struggles over the legitimacy of certain activities, practices, ways to behave can be avoided.

The fact that the reflection process on this issue simply stops because two of the three colleagues quit the job is a good reminder that there are significant influences also from spheres outside of the individual school.

27 Will They Stay or Will They Go

In a free alternative school with pre-school, primary and SEK 1 morning circle is a set feature in all age groups. A teacher in the pre-school section (2 – 6 yrs) brings up morning circle as a topic in the sectional staff meeting.

"He thought, well, isn't it dreadful to force them, well, to force them, if small children want to go, they will go anyway, you know, and you may try to hold them back, on your lap and say 'pst', but they will still go or they will be noisy and make it unbearable and you can forget about your morning circle."

The discussion then is about making morning circle a voluntary activity like the rest of the activities in the school. The teacher who took part in the interview is sceptical.

"I was not convinced at first because I thought, no, that is all right as we did it since then, and that it will all completely disperse, and the older ones will also leave, I was sceptical. I was really, really sceptical."

A compromise is negotiated. Children are obliged to come to the start of morning circle but they don't have to sit through until it is all over. It is yet at the discretion of the adults to allow children to leave.

"Such a morning circle can last quite various times. (...) And that, that they are supposed to be there when we start, you know, that they do not run around somewhere else, but that they be there at first. And when they really have enough, that we say: 'You can go to the other room and play.'"

Comment

Morning circle is a frequent topic in free alternative schools. In many cases it is in fact the only compulsory activity for children. As such it becomes a matter for discussion. This is not different in the example here. The discussion is about the freedom to decide whether or not a person wishes to participate in a group activity. This group activity is however one that is scheduled by the group leaders. It becomes a ritualised activity. The particular aspect of establishing, expressing and confirming group coherence, in terms of Bernstein/Elvin/Peters: the consensual aspect of ritual is highlighted by the teacher in the interview.

A discussion about the obligation for children to take part in the activity automatically raises the question of de-ritualisation. The lines of argument as sketched above are quite typical. The result in this case is a continuation of the ritual.

What is negotiated here is the concept of childhood that is legitimately used to define and articulate the concrete reality in the practice of the school. It is also the position of the adults in the group, the degree of control which they are supposed to exert over children (here: in the particular situation of morning circle). At the end of the day it is still in the power of the adults to decide if a child had enough or not. De-ritualising even in the form of making morning circle voluntary for children would have toppled over this position of the adults.

Or, the same to be expressed from the other side: taking away the position of the adults (remember: ritual experts) would have de-ritualisation as a likely consequence.

28 The Song's Over

In a free alternative school the teachers have decided that the singing of a song is an obligatory element of morning-circle. They explicitly include it as a ritual element that is meant to strengthen group coherence and to incite an emotional bond to the school community.

In practice the children resist the singing. They don't participate as expected, remain silent, mourn and complain about the singing. One teacher takes the children's' complaints up and brings the topic to a staff meeting. This teacher argues that the children feel compelled, that the singing is dysfunctional because they don't want it and thus will always bastardise it.

"And at some stage I said, if, if we realise and if we all realise that they don't need that, that they can't appreciate it, there is no point in forcing them only because we want it that way, you know. And there was pro and con then. Some said, the children are not yet able to understand why that is important, but we want it simply for the emotional bond to the group and so on. (...) And it was quite emotional then, too, the discussion."

She remembers two colleagues in particular getting very emotional. These colleagues find it important to stick to the ritual even if the children don't want it. The team negotiates a formula whereby 'singing will happen when it fits'.

In practice however it is more or less abandoned. It happens only occasionally when there is a birthday celebrated, but not otherwise.

Comment

The lines of argument here are quite similar as in the example before. The underlying topic is re-occurring. The teacher who took part in the interview (and advocates de-ritualisation) is in fact convinced of the value of rituals in general. She also shares the view that rituals as an expression and reinforcement of group coherence are important. Nevertheless she successfully negotiates a removal of the obligatory singing from morning-circle. For her a consensual ritual has to grow organically from the groups interaction and can not be forced per decree.

The team amongst themselves however also appease the two colleagues who feel strongly about the singing. In the formula that *"singing will happen when it fits"* their aspirations are acknowledged. Such an arrangement settles the momentary conflict that arose in the staff meeting, hence takes the cutting edge away. It yet leaves open the chance for shifting negotiations into the practical arena. With a formula like this it is left to each individual to try and convince the others in a given situation that now singing may fit, or as well not.

5.2.8. Defining Roles of Teachers in Community

Rituals in school include also those events in which school and wider community come together, social gatherings, ceremonies, festivals, public performances. Teachers inevitably play a role in these rituals. Even where a teacher decides not to take part in a particular ritual it will be noted as a statement. The teacher of the Irish primary school who does not want to attend mass outside school hours can be sure that her absence will be spoken about by parents and colleagues (… which she anticipates and consequently seeks absolution, although it is formally not necessary).

For teachers to reflect upon rituals that are located at this intersection of school and community can also mean to engage with the theme of defining the teachers' role in the community.

29 Such Drama

An Irish primary school stages a public play at Christmas time in the local community hall. It is as much a fund-raiser as it is promoting the school in the community. Afterwards the teachers discuss informally about the play.

The amount of work put in by teachers and the time used for the preparation are identified as a problem. There is agreement amongst the teachers that they would not like to continue doing the extra work every year. Also the amount of time that is lost for curriculum delivery is mentioned.

There are also arguments highlighting the value of the performances for self-esteem of children, and for community coherence, however there is consensus amongst the teachers that it is too much for them every year.

Consequently the teachers decide to have a two-year rhythm for the public performances. The decision is then also recorded in the next staff meeting.

Comment

Teachers are paid to deliver the curriculum. This is their task as far as the Department of Education is concerned. Preparing children for a public performance that is staged on a Saturday or Sunday evening is not part of the official task of the teachers. Many teachers still do that, and they cherish the social gain that lies in such engagement. This is not different in the example presented here.

However there is also an element of self-preservation on the side of the teachers that has them looking at their position within the wider school community with a focus on economic use of their energies. In the Christmas play they find themselves in a role of ritual experts for an audience that stretches far beyond the school walls.

Just as much as there are expectations on the side of 'Sister X' (example 12) and on the side of parents in the free alternative school to organise an overnight stay (example 19), there are expectations also in the example of the Christmas play. When reflecting on the event the teachers negotiate amongst themselves an acceptable definition of their role in the community. In this case the result is what the teacher in the interview presents as a form of a compromise between the lines of argument.

5.2.9. Negotiating Ritual Leadership

Events in which the wider school community is involved are favoured occasions for the hierarchical structures in a school to be displayed and at the same time confirmed or shifted. Reflection on ritual celebrations can just as well enter into a negotiation of leadership roles.

30 Winter Solstice

In a free alternative school winter solstice is celebrated every year since the day the school started.

In a staff meeting the preparation for winter solstice is discussed. The teacher who in the past had the role of leading the celebration refuses to do it again. She claims that in recent years the celebration increasingly lacks spirituality. This is expressed in parents standing aside and chatting like at a cocktail-party, they rush for food without waiting for the buffet to be officially opened, and they pay no attention to the speech/es. She puts the question to the team whether the celebration is still wanted at all.

The colleagues confirm that in fact the celebration is still wanted. The discussion then concentrates on who will take on organising it.

This discussion is repeated annually. In one year the male members of staff claim responsibility for the preparation and organisation of the celebration. The men in general follow the same script as usual. Yet the women in the staff are not happy with the result.

"Q – No, wait a second, was there not the fairy of lights, and was the bonfire lit up, was that all the same?

A – Ah well, yes, that was, ahm, they found that quite O.K. to have a script to follow. (...) But I don't know, did they change something? They had thought about the fairy and should they replace her with a dwarf or something. They wanted to include a child there, I think, at the time a child did that and it wasn't the fairy of light but rather a dwarf in a costume. But by and large it was the same structure.

Q – And what was different then?

A – The energy."

In the staff meeting after the celebration it is reflected upon and criticised for its 'lack of energy' – the men retreat and leave it up to the women again.

Comment

The gender balance of staff in this school is fifty-fifty. However the sectional leaders are all female. The move of the male members of staff to take on organising the winter solstice celebration breaks into a long time female domain.

The reflection on the course that the celebration took is immediately linked to the question who did (or will) lead it. The theme that dominates the reflection thus is ritual leadership. Obviously there are repercussions of ritual leadership also into the overall power relations amongst staff. The ritual leader and the group that is organising an event like the winter solstice celebration enjoy an increase in their informal status if the event is seen as a success.

5.2.10. Trading Tips and Tricks

A specific process concerns the trading of tips and tricks. It is particularly observable in reflection processes in which a young (new) teacher engages with an old (experienced) teacher. In the communication one of the two partners is afforded a monopoly on the correct interpretation of a given situation or topic while the other partner takes on a complementary role, this holds also for reflections on rituals.

31 Three Wise Women

A teacher who has just finished teacher training starts working in a German mainstream school. In her training she heard about the value of class-council as a means of social learning. She introduces it in her (5th) class, but she is not happy with the result.

She approaches three older colleagues (each individually) informally. She gets three different versions of class-council. She does not discuss with the older colleagues, but rather listens to them.

One of the colleagues emphasises the need for children to directly talk to each other during class-council, another one suggests a round in which green and red cards are exchanged as symbols of praise and criticism amongst the children, the third one talks about class-council as a weekly review and feedback amongst children on their behaviour during the week. Afterwards she takes on certain elements of what the colleagues have told her from their own practice, while she dismisses other elements.

Comment

Formally the older colleagues are at the same level as herself. They are class teachers just like her. In the situation that the teacher creates with her older colleagues there is yet a status difference acknowledged from the outset.

At the same time she is aware about the demarcation line of the classroom door. She constructs herself in this situation as a learner who is shopping around for advise. In this role she is able to listen to the colleagues without getting into a compromised position. In not discussing the suggestions of her older colleagues with them she keeps her autonomy in making the decision what practice to implement in her own class.

A peculiar detail in this report is that she approaches exactly those three colleagues. At other times during the interview she says of them that she could not work with them due to their views which she finds too child-centred. Yet it is exactly these colleagues whose advise she looks for.

32 Boisterous in the Bus

A teacher in an Irish primary school has developed what he calls his 'little ritual' for keeping his class calm and quiet when they are on a bus trip. At the beginning of a trip he usually goes around in the bus chatting to children individually until everyone is rather settled.

One day a trip to another town takes place but the class teacher is not in the bus. The children get boisterous. The teacher who is with them can not keep them quiet. Afterwards she reports the situation to the class teacher.

"So, we would have discussed that. The teacher, who wasn't as experienced as I would have been on buses and this was her situation and this is what happened. And she was, you know, more or less asking me to talk to the children or give out to them or whatever. So we discussed it and I just pointed out a few little things that I do when they get on a bus first. And that leads to a situation where they're calm. (...) And so she was saying to me: 'Well, normally we sit down here and they're quiet.' And I said: 'Yes, but that's because I have spent the first 15 minutes just being a presence without even having to say anything, but just being a presence down there.' (...) I mean, that's, she was, she was open to it. I mean, she would have been on a bus many times with me and probably didn't realise, probably just thought I was chatting down there or whatever, you know. Obviously didn't realise the purpose behind

it. But, so I just kind of pointed out to her that these are little sort of things that you just learn from experience."

Comment

From the interview it is not clear what the female teacher in this example makes out of the information that her colleague passes on. As a reflection process it is again a rather short affair, happening informally. In it a trick of the trade is explained by the male colleague who in his report also constructs himself as the more experienced partner in the conversation. There is no indication of any further examination either of the problematic situation in the bus or of the actual 'little ritual' that is suggested to solve it. The interpretation offered by the male colleague stands.

33 Anything but Television

In a German mainstream school 4th class has a regular morning circle every Monday. The children are asked to tell each other stories of what they did during the weekend. The class teacher is in her first year after college.

In one of the Monday morning circles a child speaks extensively about watching TV. The teacher requests that the child speaks about something different. The child starts again, but comes back to TV, does this three times before the teacher eventually asks the child to stop and somebody else to take over with a new story.

In the sectional staff meeting she brings the topic up. She explains the situation and asks for feedback.

"Yes, I mean, one of the colleagues, she is very experienced and also quite resolute. While I as a new teacher quite often still think, no, I can't do that, they are only children. But she said: 'No, once he was to start about having watched a film, I would have said: Stop! [claps her hands] Not this. I don't want to hear that you have watched television. If you have not done anything else, than that's it.'"

The young teacher argues that the circle is for telling about weekend experiences, and the child has experienced watching television. The older teacher asks: “Does it annoy you or not?” The young teacher answers: “It does.” Old teacher: “Then you need to act.”

“Q – And was there a discussion between you and the colleague (...) it sounds as if it was a rather short exchange.

A – It did not take long, that's true. There was no long discussion that I would have said: 'No, I can't do that, I see that all quite differently.' Because at the time I was not happy with the situation in class myself.”

In the next circle time she implements the rule that children shall not tell any stories about computer-games or about television.

Comment

This works for the young teacher because the older colleague wipes away the tender doubts that she had. In the short exchange between the two the younger one actually argues as she herself would expect a child to argue in a discussion with her as the teacher. But the resolute determination that the old teacher displays does the job for her. It provides the necessary back-up for her to not feel at fault implementing her anti-tv-policy. If pressed hard she can excuse herself by taking recourse on the instructive comments from her colleague. And it is possible that she uses it also in her inner dialogue when doubts (and possible feelings of guilt) nag her.

5.2.11. Review Practice Against Conceptual Ideas

There can be no educational practice without a concept: a concept that is of childhood, of learning, of justice, of truth, to name but a few aspects. Everyday practice in schools however underlies numerous influences. In the dynamic environment of a school the most honourable conceptual ideas and aspirations can easily fade away from the radar.

For teachers reflecting on rituals can pave the way to a review of practice against conceptual ideas that are promoted in the particular school. In earlier examples this was partly implicated already. The discussion about the sexualised dance performance (example 20) and the discussion about abandoning presentations in the pre-school section of a free alternative school (example 11) are the most obvious cases. In both of them the connection to conceptual elements is immediate and in the actual reflection process also made explicit amongst the teachers. One more example that illustrates this point.

34 Aspirations Overhaul

A teacher starts working in a free alternative school. In the school there is a weekly school meeting. This is an assembly of all members of staff and all children. The school meeting is a decision-making forum. It is supposed to work on the consensus principle whereby a decision requires a consensual support. The teacher however experiences the school meeting in contrast to the conceptual ideas.

"School meeting is meant to be for the children, if they have something that concerns them, they can bring it up there. If they have a problem and realise: 'That is not going right here, we need a rule or something.' Also if there is a personal conflict that can't be solved it can be brought up in the school meeting and ask for support from the other children. But in my experience the school meeting is used mainly by the adults for blazoning out things, making announcement, passing on information. (...) It is usually rather messy, too, with shouting and yelling."

The school concept stipulates that the principle of self-regulation is adhered to. For the school meeting however it is not clear whether children are obliged to take part or not. The teacher reports of children hiding when school meeting is on and colleagues chasing them to bring them into the meeting.

The practical interpretation of the consensus principle is a further problem.

"A – I find it nice, the aspiration to say, one is open for the others, is interested in their opinions and tries to achieve highest satisfaction for everyone. This is what I understand as consciousness about consensus. And I believe that comes up automatically. But it is a different story to say: 'No, we will leave the room only if we find a consensus and a vote is anyway out of the question.' (...) And this is another ritual in my opinion. It is ritualised that there is no voting, categorically.

Q – How do you know when there is a consensus?

A – Exactly this is a problem."

The teacher raises the issue of the apparent discrepancy between conceptual aspirations and practical implementation in a meeting with all staff members. In this meeting reactions are split. Some of the colleagues defend the practice as is, others agrce that there may be a need to discuss the issue in more depth. The discussion in the staff meeting remains a short exchange of opinions.

For the teacher who raised the issue the topic is not dealt with. It will be brought up again, possibly in the regular reflective supervision meetings. This process is ongoing at the time of the interview.

Comment

With a new person coming into a school there is always a new perspective coming also. This offers the chance to review the established practice against this new perspective. In this case the new teacher has made a conscious decision to work in this particular school. The school concept played an important role in the decision. Therefore it is only logical that the point of reference for the new teacher in the reflection is the school concept. The connection from observation of practice to conceptual aspirations is made immediately and is made explicit. The fact that there is a school concept in written format makes this connection easier.

5.3. Reflection as a Social Act

The extensive coverage given to the various examples over the last pages was meant to develop the themes that can be identified in the reports of teachers about reflection processes on rituals. What I am offering here is an enhanced way of understanding what goes on in these reflection processes of teachers.

What is at stake in the reflection processes is the legitimacy of certain ways of defining, articulating and shaping reality. By systematically including these elements as parameters in the analysis of the examples as reported by the teachers it is possible to demonstrate how the application of a framework based on such an enhanced understanding leads to results that transcend those to be gotten by simply applying the tools derived from theories of reflection as referred to earlier.

What the examples show is that the reality of reflection on rituals amongst teachers is not a neutral activity. And it would be hard to imagine how it could be, given that the situation in which the reflection takes place is not a neutral situation either. How reality is to be shaped depends on power relations amongst those who are involved in it. Where a particular definition, articulation or materialisation of reality is negotiated it is necessarily also a negotiation of these power relations.

This is mirrored already in models of communication theory in which the content and the relationship aspects of communication are depicted as always co-existing in each and every communication (see Watzlawick/Beavin/Jackson 1967, p 51 ff.). In the literature on rituals in schools we find this phenomenon also implied in the process of identity-bargaining (Wellendorf 1979) as referred to in chapter one.

Teachers in reflection processes engage in a situational strategic manner. They decide when it is best to bring up a topic, when not, who to approach, who not, which argument to place at a given time, which not. What we find in the examples reported by the teachers is best depicted in terms of negotiating legitimacy. Legitimacy, that is, of certain ways to interpret reality and to act accordingly. Such an understanding is not yet present in the theoretical contributions on reflection as referred to earlier.

The instruments provided by these theories are certainly not wrong. It would be possible to depict the various examples of reflection processes on rituals in terms of their processual scale. We would then find that most of the processes reported by teachers would in fact be subsumed in Griffiths/Tann's category of 'review'. To decide if there are cases of 'research' we would have to define where the threshold of systematic observation lies that distinguishes it from simple observation, or the boundary of rigorous analysis in comparison to simple analysis. We would also find that in none of the examples recourse is made to the use of what Griffiths/Tann term 'public theories'.[27] Thus we can conclude that 'retheorising' does not occur in them.

27 The only exception of this is the example in which the three parallel class teachers decide to reduce the dictations to one per semester.

It is similarly possible to categorise the reflection processes in terms of their functional character as suggested by Jack Mezirow. We then would find that there are mainly processes of content or process reflection reported, and we would not be surprised by such a finding either. It would confirm the common sense assumption that most reflection processes actually aim at finding an immediate solution for a given problem. Premise reflection, an "assessment of the validity of norms, roles, codes, 'common sense', ideologies, language games, paradigms, philosophies, or theories that we have taken for granted" (Mezirow 1991, p. 105) would be found to be a rare aspect in the examples. The discussion about the school assembly in the last example comes closest to enter into these realms. However it is not guaranteed that it will actually happen.

The implicit model in these approaches is the engagement of an individual person with a subject matter, be it the choreography of a given ritual or be it the paradigmatic concept of childhood underlying the assumption that a 5-year old needs to be forced to take part in morning circle. This engagement can not be questioned. It is self-evident that reflection will always be about some subject matter, here: a ritual activity in school.

What is missing in the models however is the conceptual inclusion of the social character of the reflection process. Not only has it implications on processual scale and functional orientation, it also directly influences the contributions made by the various participants who discuss a certain ritual activity, hence: How reality is legitimately defined and articulated in the reflection process.

In this regard the themes developed above are a way to depict the reflection of teachers in their professional environment as a social act and yet another situational strategic activity, a negotiation of legitimacy of defining, articulating and shaping reality and a negotiation of power relations.

I will pick up the issue of power again in chapter six when I turn explicitly to the idea of critical reflection. But first it is necessary to have a further look at the material gathered in the interviews.

The examples referred to so far were all about teachers reflecting with colleagues, in terms of ritual analysis: ritual experts amongst themselves.

There are yet a few examples also of reflection processes that bring together all actors involved in a given ritual. These shall be attended to next.

5.4. Collective Negotiations

For a ritual to happen it needs participants. A celebration like winter solstice may be planned and organised by a small group of ritual experts and someone may take on the role of leading the ceremony, yet without a sufficient number of participants it will simply not happen. A teacher implementing class council relies on the class to be there. Empty chairs can be put in a circle but they won't tell each other about their weekend adventures.

In some of the examples reported by teachers in the interviews the reflection processes actually take place amongst all actors, that is teachers and pupils. In all cases they are from free alternative schools in which there is a primary and secondary section. Collective negotiations can happen in two ways.

5.4.1. Transfer into Collective Negotiation via 'Uprising'

In the examples recounted above there are cases also where children don't play along in the rituals, most obvious in the various examples where children don't line up as expected. We have seen already that teachers can react to these occurrences by reflecting amongst themselves and e. g. change script and choreography of the ritual. In the interviews some cases where also mentioned in which the situation as initiated by children's interventions were transferred into a collective negotiation.

35 Saying Grace

The teachers in a free alternative school decide to have a ritual in which before meals (breakfast and lunch) all people in the room are holding hands so as to build a long chain. Then a formula of saying grace in reverence of the natural cycle is to be said ("earth who brought us this, sun who let it ripen ..."). The children in the respective group are 5/6th class.

In practice the children don't like holding hands. Adults at meal times always struggle to make the holding of hands happen. The children also claim that the formula is "silly" and suggest a different wording. In this they add one extra word each day until the formula is unspeakable.

"And also, that they felt it took too long, they wanted to start eating. And there were a couple of, really a good few complaints. At the beginning we said: 'No, that will be done, it is extremely important for us.' Ahm, until we then at some stage brought it up in a staff meeting. Because, we didn't take it serious for a long time, their criticism. The criticism of the children: 'I don't want that any more, holding hands, and I want to eat right away.' And eventually they were up in rage and said: 'I don't want that any more.'"

The team discusses the issue in a staff meeting. One colleague 'O' pushes strongly for preserving the ritual. This colleague is very religious and claims that saying grace is essentially important for each individual. He argues further that there have been other rituals already abandoned in the school in recent times and that giving up the ritual before the meal would be a blow to the community spirit. On this ground the ritual is continued.

However the children make it a topic in the weekly assembly.

"Q – And did adults take part in this discussion?

A – Yes.

Q – O.K., and the children said: 'We don't want that any more.'

A – Exactly. And the adults then have said, in this case 'O', ahm: 'But we don't want to have nothing at all. We don't want to start without anything. Let us see what we can do there.' And then they came up with a solution."

A decision is made to have a minute silence before eating.

"Q – And the solution is one of which you also said, the children would not have come up with it.

A – Well, if 'O' had not intervened, the children would have said: "We simply start once everybody is there.' Yes. Exactly."

Comment

The process comprises of a number of successive steps:

1. Ritual experts negotiate ritualisation (formalisation) of the activity before meals, this includes script and choreography. According to the teacher who took part in the interview there was no controversy about either the fact of ritualisation or about the script and choreography at this time.

2. The children in practice negotiate by sabotaging the ritual.

3. Ritual experts re-negotiate amongst themselves. At this stage the value system that is expressed in the ritual is made explicit. It is accepted as valid and the ritual is reconfirmed.

4. The children transfer the process into a collective negotiation.

5. A compromise is negotiated.

The compromise that is found in the opinion of the teacher in the interview is yet one that is based on a strong intervention of 'O'. The teacher in the interview suggests that the discrepancy of rhetoric and experience in discussion in this case is simply used to advance the adult position, in terms of numbers also the minority position.

"(...) he is a master in rhetoric, and [laughs], well that's how I know him, if he has an opinion then he pushes it a hundred percent, bullying his way through regardless, and he takes whatever arguments he finds and throws them in for good measurement, and yet you know that it is really only his opinion, and his own agenda that is so strong behind it."

The discussion in the weekly assembly in this way is in itself another negotiation of power relations. Expressed in the terminology as introduced above the collective negotiation deals with the themes of de-ritualisation (from the side of the children), and adaptation of the script of the ritual. The theme of de-ritualisation is not accepted by the teacher. The children don't pursue it after his intervention, they rather meet him on the theme of adapting the script.

36 Sleep and Chat

In a free alternative school there are different morning circles on offer with different adults. The children can choose to take part in any of them or also in none.

One of the teachers creates a choreography for morning circle in reflection with a colleague. The idea is to *"make people active"* by playing a game, singing a song or other activity during morning circle.

Children take part but do not bring in any activities themselves. After a while the teacher also stops bringing up activities but rather concentrates on making announcements. The children say that they don't really like the format. When the teacher is away on a course, the children create a new format. They have a *"sleep and chat circle."* These children are mainly 5/6th class.

"It didn't take that long for it to be discussed in the first place, I'd say maybe a month at the most because it becomes quite immediately apparent that things aren't, that people maybe aren't satisfied in the way you're doing it, and so as I say, suggested changes. Ahm, I think with this sleeping and chatting thing that came about, it (...) that was, it's been not that long, it was before the Christmas holidays, so it must have been two months, three months or something. And I was away on a course, training thing, and I wasn't there one Friday, and I came back in the next week, I went to go to morning circle and the kids said to me: 'We don't actually need you. We worked out how we do morning circle and it's really nice. And what we're doing is this.' And I said: 'Oh, am I allowed to join in then.' And they said: 'Oh yeah, you can join in.' [laughs] And so it actually came about that way, it came about that way, there was one day were they were on their own, and they created what they, what they wanted. (...)

And then they allowed me to come and join it, and then we worked out from there how it would actually work. And now it's quite like, they chat with me. They know that it's important to me that if there's things that I would think a need to be announced within the space, that I do say them. Because I think it's important, I feel like it's important, it's my responsibility if there's an important meeting going on or whatever that they know about it. And they, and we've then talked about the fact that that's important for me and I need that and so, they do, we arrive and it's time for 'Sleep-Chat-Round' but they also say: 'Anything you really needing to tell us today? This is your moment.' [laughs] And they give me that space because I've expressed that that's my, that's my need when I come there as well. And I respect their needs for what they want to do there, but we try and work out so that both (..)"

Comment:

It is obvious how the opening of the space for the children creates a situation in which they take charge of the ritual. Subsequent to the earlier notion of ritual ownership one can say that here the children appropriate the ritual in the absence of the teacher. In this sense they effectively negotiate their position in the constellation with the teacher.

On her return she accepts the shifted positions. On this basis then there is a reflection as collective negotiation initiated about the different ambitions that are connected with the idea of morning circle. A new choreography is mutually agreed.

5.4.2. Collective Negotiation from the Start

The second way that collective negotiation of rituals happens is where reflection is started as a collective process from the very start.

37 No Visitors

In a free alternative school a daily morning circle is held. The age of the children in the group is 10 – 14. The teacher observes that at some stage the morning circle becomes a rather dull thing and children are not engaging in conversation any more as they did before.

He has a hunch that this may be caused by the presence of visitors, mainly students who are in the school for practical parts of their teacher training. He discusses the topic with the children.

"And I suggested, O.K., let us reserve one day in the week where no visitors are allowed during morning circle. And they were all up for it on

the spot, and they said: 'That's what we do.' And we picked a day and so, we have morning circle for ourselves once a week, and the quality changed immediately."

Comment

The example may seem minor due to its briefness. There is yet a lot in it. One may say that as far as reflection is concerned there is not much happening, in fact it is the teacher reflecting on the situation on his own (a process of thought without exchange with anyone) first and him doing so is not at all a collective effort. That is true. Yet, it is the fact that he brings his thoughts into exchange in discussion with the children that gives the reflection any sort of relevance. His thoughts would have made as much difference to the course of the world as an unwritten poem did he not do anything about them.

The school runs on a principle where in matters that concern the group each member has one vote irrespective of age, that is children and adults alike. In this environment for the teacher to act on his thoughts the logical consequence is to bring it to the children with whom he shares morning circle.

The teacher here does what David Gribble describes as sharing responsibility: "Democratic decision-making in schools does not mean adults abandoning their responsibility, it means adults sharing their responsibility with younger people. As long as this sharing is genuine, and group decisions cannot be overturned at the whim of the head teacher or the governors, teachers will find their relationship with their pupils transformed and the atmosphere in the classroom co-operative rather than confrontational" (Gribble 2012).

Despite its brevity the rather brief exchange in which the teacher and the children conclude to have a day for themselves every week is yet a collective negotiation. It is a reflection process that can be depicted in terms of processual scale (review) and functional character (content). But more to the point it is a social act, one that in itself does far more than generating knowledge. It influences the social situation strongly. It confirms the shared ritual ownership of children and teacher of the morning circle. It demonstrates to the children that the adult actually cares for the common well-being of the group. With this little exchange group coherence is effectively (re-)established, the consensual ritual defended against a possible dilution.

As for community spirit: how much more effective is this small act – in comparison to the laboured efforts to establish group coherence via coercive participation!

38 Re-structuring Juridical Committee

A free alternative school expands from primary only to include SEK 1. Due to the increase in the number of people populating the school the school assembly, that is all teachers and all children (age range from 6 - 14), discuss the format of their juridical committee. A decision is made to re-structure the committee. Two teachers are allocated the task to mediate the process of re-structuring.

The two teachers (one of them is the partner in the interview) reflect on the way *"to find a solution for re-structuring"* and come up with a seminar for all potential candidates. In the seminar discussion ensues about the composition of the juridical committee, about the qualities that are required of members of the committee and about the actual choreography for meetings of the juridical committee. This concerns quite detailed aspects, too:

"We thought about the seating order and what it does to someone. We asked two participants to leave the room and then we asked them to come in for three times in a row. Every time we had changed the seating order. (...) First there was a room with a lot of distraction where people sat in different areas of the room. Then we made it into a setting like in a court hearing, with a table and behind the table the members of the committee, and the plaintiff and the defendant on chairs in front of the table. And then we also made an open circle of chairs with free chairs for the two who came in.

And then after they did that three times we asked them about their feelings in the different situations. And, yes, simply to think about, O.K., what does such a seating order actually do to oneself. And, ahm, it was clear then that we needed a different room (...) where it was possible to sit in a circle. And this is how we do it now."

Participants in the seminar are all those people who declared an interest in being a member of the juridical committee at some stage.

"Q – That means in the seminar not only those took part who were elected to the committee, but rather the entire pool of children?

A – Correct. And the adults, they had to take part, too."

Comment

In the seminar children and adults together and collectively negotiate the script and choreography of the ritual. Their authority to decide on this is directly derived from the assembly in which the democratic principle of one person one vote is adhered to irrespective of age.

The entire process is best described in terms of collective negotiation, here: on (re-)structuring a central ritual of school governance.

5.5. Where Reflection on Rituals Does Not Happen

In the material presented so far there were a number of examples where reflection processes were stopped at a certain point. The teacher who strategically holds back in the staff meeting when she feels that there is no winning of an argument on lining up is one of them. The case in which discussion about abandoning dictation stops because an external expert is deemed to be stupid is another one. Other reflection processes were incredibly short (small in scale). This concerns situations like the brief exchanges on children telling stories about television in circle time or the ritualisation of dismissal. Hence one could argue that in such cases reflection did not happen.

This however would mean drawing a line at the wrong point. In all the above mentioned examples there was at least some exchange about an activity that the respective teacher identified as a ritual or ritualised activity. In this sense a process of reflection was initiated. That it stopped in some cases very soon afterwards does not do away with the fact that it started.

The following passages refer to those activities, depicted as rituals, that are not brought up by the teachers as a topic in a reflection process with others in their professional practice. Consequently in these cases no reflection with others happens at all.

5.5.1. Religious Hegemony

The most obvious area in which reflection of rituals does not happen for teachers in the three different school types concerns the entire complex of religion in Irish school. Irish teachers associate the term ritual first and foremost with religion. In the course of the interviews there were numerous situations where religious rituals in schools came up in the conversation. In only two of them reflection took place: the teacher who does not want to attend mass outside school hours and the undercover rumblings about the extra work due to confirmation. In all other cases religious rituals were not reflected upon.

For teachers who themselves are religious a religious ritual in school will not be an issue to reflect upon. They grew up with them, they are practised in each and every school. It is just 'normal'.

"Q - You said that religious rituals are actually quite common in your school, as in that's day to day practice. Have they ever been discussed? Or reflected upon?

A - Not really, because, I mean, we were brought up going to school and doing our three prayers. That continued, and we were, we do the Alive-O-program which isn't in the curriculum. So we all had to do a separate course in college to teach religion. So, it's not really discussed, you just kinda take out your book and go with it, like." (IPS 03)

With 96 % of all schools under religious patronage, there is no questioning of religious ritual. *"No, I wouldn't, my colleague and I would never have discussed, well, should we [laughing: you know, should we throw it out the window], or whatever, it's just, we'd, we just know it's part and parcel in a catholic school as such, you know, that one does these things as such."* (IPS 08)

The hegemonic position of the catholic church within the education system in Ireland over decades clearly echoes in these accounts. However "over recent decades, Irish society has been undergoing major political, social, economic, cultural, demographic and educational change. Among key changes (...) are the greater diversity of religious belief systems and the more multicultural composition of the population. There is also a minority of about 10 percent who declare themselves as having 'no religion'" (DES 2012, p. 1).

Teachers who have broken away from religion are still obliged to teach the religious belief system in their school. This brings them in a dilemma situation.

"I, it's an area that I would, I think it's a lot of bunkum, it's a lot of rituals. Listen now, if you want to go rituals, definitely you are in the right zone there, and I think there's a lot of people who are fed up of doing, following the rituals, and I'd be one of them. I just, I'm not a ritualistic person at the moment. I have kind of broken away, this is, on the record, off the record or whatever, I just, I would have no time for it, any of that. I would call it rubbish. But I will do it on a professional basis, because I'm expected to. (...) But yes. I would have no time for any of those religious rituals. On a personal basis. On a professional basis I would go through it, do you know. I'm being the [laughing: the biggest hypocrite.] You know, I be a hypocrite if it's part of my contract." (IPS 04)

From the interviews it is quite evident that questioning religion as such in the context of a school under religious patronage is a no-go-area. During the interviews the Irish teachers inevitably also speak about various aspects of school life that are related to religion. I wish to briefly divert and attend to two examples in this context here.

39 Santa Claus

In an Irish primary school there is only one child in the infant classes who comes from a non-catholic family. This child tells the classmates that Santa Claus does not exist. The other children get upset. A teacher meets with the mother of the child and discusses the issue.

"Well, the parent of the child was saying, that, look, this is a lie and you shouldn't be, you know fostering a lie or, you know. And my argument was that it wasn't really a lie, it was, you know, I suppose,

whether you call it a ritual or what, but it's a tradition and a custom and it's a harmless sort of, and it's a nice thing and so on. (...)

The discussion ended in that we both agreed to respect one another's viewpoint, that the child was quite entitled obviously not to believe in Santa Claus or whatever, but that we would appreciate if she just sort of, she wouldn't be talking to the other children about it. And if there is any other aspect of her faith, you know, that would be different, that we would respect that as long as she would sort of respect ours as well."

This example was actually depicted by the teacher as a reflection process. In line with the standards applied throughout my study I agree with the teacher. On the other side the reflection (here in form of negotiating of non-conforming position) is not really about a ritual in school. Santa Claus is not celebrated in the school either. The reflection between the teacher and the mother is a reflection about the reflection on the ritual that the children have.

40 National Anthem

In an Irish primary school the class gets up three times a day to say a catholic prayer. 40 % of the children in the class are not catholic. One of the prayers is said at the end of the school day.

"Q - And who speaks?

A - They all do. Obviously not the children who, the children who aren't catholic don't. Just the catholic children would say prayers. And I would say it with them at the same time.

Q - And you say you have non-catholic children in the school there.

A - Oh yes, yes.

Q - And what do they do at the time?

A - They just, they just stand at their place, while we're waiting to say prayers.

Q - Right, O.K., and they wait for the prayers to be said, because that's officially the end of the school day?

A - Yes. But they're also, I would also say to them, if they want to say their own prayer from their own religion, they're allowed to do that, like, if they wanted.

Q - Does it ever happen?

A - Aahm, not out loud, but some definitely, children, some Muslim children would bow their heads, and they would say their own, I don't know I've never, they've never asked could they say it out. I was not having a problem with them saying it out. They do sometimes have their own little quiet time."

At the same time the children in this class have successfully negotiated the end of school day ritual. Apart of the obligatory prayer there is also a singing of the Irish national.

"A - Aahm, we do our tidy up, we get ready for prayers, say prayers, and then sometimes, not every single day, but a lot of days they will ask, can they sing it. Like they ask, I don't, I don't make them, it will come from them, not from me. (...) Aahm, they learned it at the start of the year and they became very patriotic about it, my class. Even though, fifty percent of them are not nationals, not non-nationals but foreign nationals. (...)

Q - But you don't raise the flag in the classroom?

A - Nonono, no. They do stand up with their hands behind :

Q - What do they do with their hands?

A - They put them behind their backs. They stand up straight and kind of push their chests out a little bit, they're quite proud of it."

What both examples have in common is the fact that they make evident how much non-conforming beliefs in Irish primary schools can have no voice. This applies to children and teachers alike. We have already seen how teachers can be afraid to openly question the role of religion in schools. There may be corridor complaints and undercover rumblings but it would not come up in a formal setting like staff meetings.

The children in the second example however find a way to effectively negotiate the situation and introduce a counter-element to the display of catholic hegemony. Paying tribute to the Irish state for them is a way to overcome the apparent separation along religious lines. The national anthem obviously has a symbolic value that they can salute in unity. How much they exchange like for like is a discussion that would lead to far away from my topic and therefore needs to be left for another time. For the teacher neither the ritual of singing the national anthem, nor in particular the religious elements were ever reflected with anyone.

In the interviews with German teachers in both mainstream and free alternative schools the complex of religion does not play a significant role. Only in one example reported by them religious motives come into play. The negotiation about saying grace before meals shows how the teacher who requests this practice on religious grounds has to actually argue his case against strong resistance.

Saying this does not mean that there are no influences of religion on the activities in schools in Germany. Conflicts about religious symbols in Bavarian classrooms that made headlines in recent years are a good indicator that education in school is still a contested field in which religious parties invest a great deal of energy. At the end of the day in Germany school and religion are defined as two separate zones of life. And yet there are ties. The first day of school that is reflected upon by teachers in example 16 for children of Christian belief also includes attending a mass. However the school has officially nothing to do with this mass. It is organised by the local church and it is the parents who will bring the children to it, sit through it and then bring the children to school to take part in the celebration that is organised by the teachers. Thus for the teachers the mass is not a question to consider when they reflect upon the welcome ceremony.

Religion can also be a point of reference like in the winter solstice celebration in the free alternative school which is clearly understood as an alternative to the Christian tradition of celebrating Christmas. According to the teacher in the interview when the event was planned the very first time the idea of connecting to pagan traditions was essential part of the plan. In the reflection processes reported by the teacher this motif however is not explicitly picked up.

In relation to reflection processes of teachers on rituals the bottom line is that there is a hegemonic position of the church in Irish education that is not mirrored in Germany. And with this hegemony institutionalised in the schools there is a taboo zone for reflection on religious rituals even for teachers who have made their personal break with the church.

5.5.2. The Done Thing

Apart of the religious rituals there are other ritual aspects of school life that are often not reflected upon because they simply seem too normal. The teacher in the earlier example on ritualisation of dismissal has at least a vague memory that at some stage she started the practice of lining up children on school tours. In many cases such a memory is not even present. *"Every class has, I think we just got them to line up, since, you line them up, that's what, that's what we've done, like in my eight years here, that was the done (...)"* (IPS 04)

Attending to the ambiguous symbolic representation in lining up and circle time reference was made to the need in the early days of institutional pedagogy to actually establish the practice of lining up children. The constant perpetuation can lead to the normalising of ritualised practice to the degree where it is beyond the radar for reflection. Circle time has the potential to become one of these ritualised practices that in the future may be far beyond questioning and simply accepted as the done thing. In the eyes of future generations of teachers who as children where exposed to circle time already it may be a case of seeing circle time as something that was always done.[28]

In many respects we all adhere to certain conventions within our daily lives that are never questioned. We dress in a certain manner, we adhere to certain hygienic standards, we wait at the yellow line in the post office to be called to the counter, we say, "How are you?" although we are not a bit interested in "how" you are. But it doesn't matter because you will not take a bit of notice of the fact that we asked you how you are. Most likely you will even return the favour and ask us a similarly conventional question, also not expecting an answer.

It is only where there is a break in the convention that it may come up for questioning. Particularly those ritual activities that are small in scale,

28 In this context see also Catherine Bell's passages on the "Construction of Tradition" (Bell 1992, p. 118 ff).

everyday rituals (Wellendorf), low rituals (Henry) are exercised habitually. We have seen in earlier examples how disturbances in the performance do actually lead to reflection. The mess created by children who don't stay in line after break time brings the topic on the agenda. For an occurrence during a ritual performance to be noted as disturbance, this occurrence also has to cross a certain threshold. It needs to be depicted as disturbance in the first place.

Conforming to conventions is normal. For it being normal it is not reflected upon as long as everyone conforms and no-one makes it into a problem. In another Irish primary school children line up always in separate lines of boys and girls. The girls are always first to go, the boys wait. This teacher also refers to this as being an *"established practice."*

"Q - And is that a part that comes up in discussion?

A - It would be established practice. To say we would have specifically, it would be probably not overly discussed about it, but it would be taken as established practice. You know what I mean, it's kind of man and woman walk to the door, you go first or I go first, we don't talk about it. But it would have been established. Maybe it's societal, do you know what I mean, that we take, it would be taken as a given. (...) To say that we categorically discussed it in the staff room I can't honestly say that we did, no.

Q - So you didn't bring it up and nobody else?

A - No, but it would be, it would be done in all classes at the same time, if you understand what I mean."

And it is not the case that the teacher would not be aware of the potential for reflecting this practice.

"I suppose maybe you could perceive it as being sexist that the girls always go first. Probably because, I suppose maybe in greater society it's always perceived as good manners from the male perspective to allow the girls out the door first or whatever. And, that, you know, it maybe gives the lads a, maybe, hopefully a little bit more respect for girls." (IPS 05)

However in the situation with the colleagues the topic is not touched. As the done thing it is simply not a topic.

5.5.3. *Demarcation Lines*

Rituals can differ from one class to another in a given school. Teachers in reflection can work on the theme of harmonising practice, and non-conforming positions can be negotiated. But in mainstream schools there is at all times the demarcation line of the classroom door that can present an impassable barrier. It is an essential part of teachers' professional status that they are the sole responsible person for whatever happens in the classroom.

"The self-contained classroom ... is more than a physical reality, for it refers to a social system, a set of recurrent and more or less permanent social relationships. Under this arrangement the teacher is separated from immediate supervision, and intrusion in this private domain is prevented by a set of understandings subscribed to by administrative officers and teacher colleagues. A set of norms exist which act to buttress the ecological separation:

(1) the teacher should be free from interference of other adults while teaching,

(2) teachers should be considered and treated as equals, and

(3) teachers should act in a non-intervening but friendly manner towards one another" (Lortie, in: Denscombe 1985, p. 70).

As we have seen the negotiation of the demarcation line is a re-occurring theme in mainstream schools in reflection processes on rituals. The sharpness of confrontation that is possible in discussion about those rituals that happen in common spaces is rarely mirrored when it comes to reflecting classroom activities. The "non-intervening but friendly manner" is usually adhered to in reflections on the latter.

The professional code of non-intervention is a type of non-aggression pact. On these grounds it is possible for teachers in mainstream schools to operate widely without reflecting at all with others on their classroom practice. Where a school hosts more than one class per year a teacher may have to adhere to a minimum standard of coordination in relation to curriculum delivery. There may be a need to agree book lists, timing of tests etc. with parallel class teachers. However all aspects of classroom culture, routines, rituals may be simply not reflected at all with others.

41 Good Morning Horse

A teacher in a German mainstream school has established in her classroom a greeting ritual. As the first thing every morning she takes up a hand puppet in the shape of a horse. The children all stand at their tables. She then plays the horse to say good morning to each child individually: good morning Patricia, good morning Patrick etc. Each child sits down after her/his name has been called. She explains why she introduced this ritual.

"A - Well, I hate it when they all together say: 'Good morning, Mrs. T.' That makes me shiver, I find it terrifying [laughs].

Q – And what is so terrifying about it?

A – Mmmh, that is, it's more like old school. [laughing: I suppose, it's a bit old-fashioned]. I don't like it. And some have it that they let the children say: 'Good morning, Mrs. Anyone, nice to have you here.' I find that all too artificial, you see, there are always some who don't find it nice to have me here at all, they would rather stay in bed if they could."

In her class then she introduces a choreography that is set off from what she perceives as old style. In doing so she does not confer with anyone. She is the one who makes the decision, there is no interference from colleagues. Her reasons are not communicated either. Reflection on the matter is not happening.

"Q – Do you know how it is done in other classes?

A – Yes, it is mostly the teacher saying: 'Good morning;' and the children all together answering: 'Good morning.'

Q – And that is different in your class.

A – Mmh.

Q – And did you talk with anyone about your reasons for doing it this way?

A – No. [laughs]

Q – You don't have any exchange on the matter?

A – No."

In her classroom she has introduced a new style in contrast to what she perceives as the old style in other classes in the school. Reflecting with colleagues about the different choreographies bears the potential to step over the line of "non-intervening and friendly manner" that is part of the non-aggression pact. She fares well in her own little empire. As long as the others leave her alone, she leaves them alone. Despite the fact that she hates the old style she will not rock the boat with her colleagues.

The theme of demarcation lines does not appear in the interviews with teachers of free alternative schools. This is however not surprising if we consider the character of these schools. The classroom door as demarcation line simply does not exist in them. Earlier I wrote about free alternative schools (example 26): When working together with the same children in the same rooms harmonisation of practice is a must, at least to the point where constant struggles over the legitimacy of certain activities, practices, ways to behave can be avoided.

Furthermore in free alternative schools it is regularly the case that children pick their activities according to their own interests, and in doing so are not restricted to one room only. Hence the standards of behaviour are carried from one to another room also, discrepancies of standards are an immediate issue for everyone involved. There is no chance for an old style and a new style to co-exist in a free alternative school.

One might assume that the professional code as depicted above applies across the board for mainstream schools. I would hold that this is in fact the case. From personal experience on management level in an Irish primary school and from several personal contacts with Irish primary teachers I can only confirm that there is no intervention in the inner affairs of teachers amongst themselves. It is interesting then to see that the theme of demarcation lines is similarly absent in the interviews with teachers of Irish primary schools.

This has to be seen in the light of what was said earlier about the ritual cultures in the three different school types. Taking rituals as indicators for the norms, values, beliefs that are enacted in a school we found that the situation of teachers in German mainstream schools is the least clear. These schools could be depicted as an environment in which the ritual culture indicates a situation in which contradictory value systems, norms, beliefs are represented in the daily practice of the schools. Irish primary schools and free alternative schools in contrast are environments in which a rather consistent system of values, norms, beliefs can be observed. Taking the teachers as ritual experts we find that teachers in Irish schools establish a rather homogeneous ritual culture. The old style and the new style that is prevalent in German mainstream schools in Ireland is largely one style, at least until now and to a degree that makes the development of the theme of demarcation lines in reflection processes unlikely.

5.6. Reflection on Rituals – Strategic Assessments

Do teachers reflect on rituals in school? Can the process of reflection be described? Can typical patterns be identified in the professional reflection processes of teachers in primary schools concerning rituals/ritualisations? These questions were raised earlier.

The extensive coverage given to the concrete examples as reported by teachers shows that it is possible to address these questions in a comprehensible way. For the requested description of the reflection processes it was helpful to employ rubrics that depict a number of themes that are developed in the reflection processes. I have pointed out already that these rubrics are not understood as a typology of pure categories into which the various examples can be neatly placed. They are merely descriptive tools which allow one to express that what has been inexpressible so far.

In each process there can be more than one theme at play. In many cases a given example could be referred to in more than one rubric. This is a consequence of the multi-layered nature of the processes. As processes of negotiation involving a number of actors whose aims are not necessarily similar, and who in fact may follow strategies aiming at different aspects of the underlying subject matter, there is always the possibility to develop the one or the other theme more pronounced in a given reflection process. Example 35 (saying grace) was presented above as a case of transfer into collective negotiation, in it there are also detectable themes of de-ritualisation or discussing ritual choreography. In example 4 (talk without consequences) demarcation lines are a dominant feature, however in it there is obviously at the same time the topic of negotiating harmonised practice. In the discussion of the teachers about the non-conforming position of the child in example 7 (special needs pave a way out) the question of harmonising practice is similarly present.

By using the suggested rubrics as descriptive tools it was possible to identify certain patterns in the reflection processes on rituals. These allow us to see how the negotiations of legitimacy are actually put into practice in the three different school types. Reflection on rituals remains a practice in which teachers engage mostly amongst themselves. This applies to all three school types. When it comes to rituals and ritualisations thus the negotiations about legitimate forms of defining and articulating, eventually shaping reality are a domain of the teachers which they mostly don't share with other partners (parents, but especially children).

Only a minority of cases from the free alternative schools refer to collective negotiations and these examples are of negotiations with children who are at the upper end of the age scale of primary school (5/6th class) in schools where there is also a secondary section included. This observation raises questions about the claim of free alternative schools as *schools of negotiation* (Scholz) as mentioned earlier. When it comes to rituals and ritualisations: What exactly are the forms of negotiation that take place between adults and children in free alternative schools?

The specific situation in Ireland, with the hegemony of the church in education, filters through also in relation to reflection processes on rituals. Religious rituals in Irish primary schools are in general not reflected upon. This despite the fact that they can be perceived as a nuisance within a school context that is gearing towards delivery of a curriculum that is focussed on the 'three R', reading, writing, arithmetic – or in more contemporary terms: literacy and numeracy.

The situation in German mainstream schools, with rather varied conceptual orientations being frequently present amongst staff within one school, accounts for a distinct focus on the theme of demarcation lines in this context. This can lead to non-reflection. It can also mean that in reflection processes the theme of demarcation is developed in a way that is not observable in the reports from Irish teachers and from teachers in free alternative schools.

The actors in the reflection processes are bound to the social situation in which they reflect. What they do or not do, the topics which they happily develop or drop, the thoughts which they exchange or censor away, the remarks which they make or hold back depends on this situation. In this regard we see how the ritual culture of a school correlates with the reflection processes that are happening in it. At the same time the actors in reflection processes are yet actors. They assess the situation in which they are and on that basis they make strategic decisions about entering into a discussion or not, drawing a demarcation line, playing a friendly non-intervention game or harmonise their practice.

The subject matter in reflections on rituals or ritualisations are social acts that are essentially linked to social order, norms, values. In Catherine Bells terminology "ritualisation is a strategic play of power, of domination and resistance, within the arena of the social body" (Bell 1992, p. 204). The exploration of the reflection processes reported by the teachers in their interviews has led to me repeatedly referring to the character of these processes as negotiations of legitimacy of certain ways of defining, articulating or materialising reality. The analysis of the examples clearly shows that these negotiations are not in the first place guided by a deliberative rationality but rather by strategic assessments of the social situation in which they take place.

Strongly resonating in these reflection processes is the particular character of rituals and ritualisations as inherently linked to the motif of power negotiations. Essential for those negotiations that are understood as ritualisation "is simultaneously the avoidance of explicit speech and narrative" (Bell 1992, p. 111). We saw earlier that a particular strand of reflection aims specifically at uncovering mechanisms at work in social situations that are normally not made explicit. Covert hegemonic assumptions and power relations are the main focus for reflection processes understood as critical reflection.

In the next chapter I will turn to this particular approach in which the motif of power takes central stage.

Chapter 6 Critical Reflection on Rituals in School

Three models of classifying reflection processes were sketched earlier: processual scale, functional character and orientational character. The last one refers to the concept of critical reflection. Stephen Brookfield's proposals can function as a point of reference in this regard.

Critical reflection in the sense of Stephen Brookfield implies that those who come together for reflection have made a decision that this is what they do:

- externalise power relations,
- investigate power relations,
- uncover hegemonic assumptions.

Externalising power relations basically means to lay them bare in a process of naming them. Investigating power relations would require a systematic analysis of these relations to find out how they are exercised, why they are there in the first place, how legitimate they are in this form etc. Externalising and investigating power relations rely on a concept of power to be used as a screening filter to be laid over the matter reflected upon.

Uncovering hegemonic assumptions means to consciously search for the roots of personal theories or common sense theories which implies that there is from the outset an assumption that these theories are possibly distorted. It further suggests a validation of these theories, why else would one want to uncover them otherwise?

As is obvious from the various examples of reflection processes on rituals as collected in the interviews with the teachers in three different school types, they are not initiated for the purpose of externalising and investigating power relations, or to uncover hegemonic assumptions. They are initiated for purposes that are clearly anchored in the practical activities of the teachers' professional lives. What the teachers look for in the reflection processes is not in the first place a (better) understanding of power relations as acted out or symbolically represented in ritual performances. It is neither an uncovering of hegemonic assumptions that allow for ritual practices being enacted in schools.

What they look for in the reflection is a practical outcome, a harmonisation of practice, a de-ritualisation, a certain choreography. These are all material results. They have practical effects and consequences: a teacher does not have to shout at children to stand in a line but rather can sit relaxed in her classroom and wait for the children to come in after break on their own; a teacher can hit against a sound-bowl and 25 children will be quiet; a teacher will stand on a stage expressing a welcome to 120 parents whose children start school on this Monday (and the local paper will have her picture printed in the local news on Friday); a teacher will eventually be able to stop grabbing the 4-year old child who can't sit still during morning circle.

From the perspective of the individual teacher this is what the professional reflection processes on rituals are about: a certain way to shape reality. The reflection is only a means to achieve this. As far as externalisation, investigation of power relations and uncovering of hegemonic assumptions are happening in a reflection process they are a means to an end. They are moves employed by a teacher or teachers in the concrete situation in which definition and articulation of reality is negotiated. The metaphorical figure of the knowledge-seeker who engages in reflection for the sake of a better understanding alone is a myth that is mocked by the actual practice in the real life situation of educational institutions.

Surely it is possible to think of reflection processes on rituals in school that are designed from the outset as critical reflection. However in the professional reflection processes of teachers on rituals that are observable at this point of history in the real situation in the three school types this is not the case. Critical reflection here is merely an *aspect* that may enter into a reflection process. If it does it is on the basis of teachers asking critical questions.

Not all questions about power relations or hegemonic assumptions are critical questions. We remember Foucault's notion of the critical attitude as mentioned in the section on critical reflection. The perpetually raised question is: "How not to be governed *like that,* by that, in the name of those principles, with such and such objectives in mind and by means of such procedures, not like that, not for that, not by them" (Foucault 1997, p. 44).

Therefore a question like: 'What power relations can be observed in this or that ritual in our school?' is an ordinary question. What makes it a critical question is the critical attitude, that is an anti-authoritarian agenda (or at least an impulse). Following such an agenda the critical investigation of power relations and hegemonic assumptions aims on scrutinising their legitimacy. Where basic assumptions are found to lack substance, or in fact to be wrong those rituals that are based on them lose their legitimacy.

As a pre-condition for critical questioning there has to be a critical attitude. And yet for a teacher having a critical attitude does not guarantee that critical reflection on rituals takes place. We found that in reflection processes teachers make strategic decisions about entering into a discussion or not. Critically externalising (naming) power relations, asking questions about them or putting hegemonic assumptions up for scrutiny are no exception of this rule. A teacher with a critical attitude will strategically decide to bring these questions up or not.

As far as rituals are the matter to be reflected upon we deal with material acts of material actors. In rituals social norms, values, belief systems are enacted. The actors who take part negotiate, by means of ritualisation, what is legitimate and what is not. They practically define and articulate reality. They do so by situational strategic interventions.

For teachers to reflect upon rituals in school is not like a film in cinema or a play in theatre, where they sit back and watch it or walk out of the show if it becomes too scary or too boring. The teachers are *in* the film, they are *on* the stage. Their every act is part of the further development of the plot. That is also why their reflection is similarly an act that is connected to other acts.

What's more about this particular drama is that in contrast to a film or to theatre there is no director and no screenplay. Directing and screenplay are constantly negotiated by the actors. In doing so they are bound to yesterdays acts, they can not simply cut and start somewhere else. This would be possible only by leaving the stage altogether. If they want to cut while on stage, they have to clean up the mess of the past while still being on stage. Their reflections are part of the film in which they play. Even while they reflect they develop the plot *on stage*. The reflection processes on rituals that are reported by the teachers in their interviews are as much determined by the system of power relations that are otherwise acted out and negotiated in the rituals.

In the rituals the actors are constantly concerned with positioning themselves in a social situation. They enact power relations, make them material. One can say they *make power happen*. "Power exists only when it is put into action (...) In itself the exercise of power is not violence; nor is it a consent which, implicitly, is renewable. It is a total structure of actions brought to bear upon possible actions; it incites, it induces, it seduces, it makes easier or more difficult; in the extreme it constrains or forbids absolutely, it is nevertheless always a way of acting upon an acting subject or acting subjects by virtue or their acting or being capable of action. A set of actions upon other actions" (Foucault 1982, p. 789).

Enacting power relations implies exerting authority, making others do, or refrain from doing. In doing so the actors are also responsible. Asking questions with an anti-authoritarian agenda or impulse about actors acting in ritualisations means to also make explicit how responsibility is located in the actors.

Earlier I referred to Catherine Bell who said that ritualisation "(…) is a way of acting that sees itself as *responding* to a place, event, force, problem, or tradition. It tends to see itself as the natural or appropriate thing to do in the circumstances. Ritualisation does not see how it actively creates place, force, event, and tradition, how it redefines or generates the circumstances to which it is responding" (Bell 1992, p. 109). Obviously it is not ritualisation that sees itself responding to a place, event, force, problem or tradition. It is the actors who see themselves responding. In doing so they shift responsibility to the initiating phenomenon. The own actions are constructed as a response. The responsibility lies on the side of the place, event, force, problem or tradition. Critically investigating rituals implies uncovering the responsibility of the actors for their actions. It makes explicit what was meant to be not explicit. This also threatens to destroy the legitimacy of one's own actions as natural and appropriate thing to do in the circumstances.

Is there evidence of critical questions aiming at externalising and investigating power relations, uncovering hegemonic assumptions in the examples reported by the teachers in the interview series? Let us have a glance at the three different school types.

Irish Primary Schools

The only example from Irish primary schools that could be assumed to name (externalise) power relations concerns the corridor talk of teachers (example 13) about the influence of religion in school. The report of the teacher is not clear on this, but it can at least be reasonably construed that in the informal discussions there may be some naming of the actual power structure that causes the burden of extra-work for the teachers. From the interview however there is no indication how explicitly this is done.

In none of the reported processes is there an attempt of uncovering of hegemonic assumptions. Where ritual practices like lining up, dismissal, honouring of past-pupil achievements, the Christmas play come up in the discussions there is no search for the roots of the 'personal theories' or 'common sense theories' that are underlying their implementation.

Power as a screening filter is not applied in any of the examples either. This concerns particularly the role of adults as decision-makers and the legitimacy of this role.

German Mainstream Schools

In the majority of cases power relations are not explicitly made an issue in these reflection processes. Only in some examples they play a role.

In the discussion about the sexualised dance performance (example 20) the fit of various value systems is discussed. The value systems themselves are not scrutinised. According to the parameters set by the institutional context the teachers make their decision to introduce a censoring agent. The power issues that are included are not investigated.

For the reflection process on the seating order (example 1) the teacher reports that the question of adults regulating the physical matters of children is actually looked at for the potential of exercising undue authority.

The teacher who holds back with her position against the lining up (example 3) holds in her hands a key to initiating critical questioning. She decides not to try to use it at the time. She expects that it won't open the door that needs to be opened.

One may argue that the teacher who has her doubts about restricting talk about television (example 33) in some way asks the question how legitimate her practice is. Yet the question is not asked explicitly and definitely not critically. I will take up this example soon again.

Free Alternative Schools

The discussion about making 'presentations' in the school with the 'non-directive' concept (example 11) involves a questioning of conceptual elements. One may argue that this is also questioning assumptions that can be seen as hegemonic, e. g. of children's needs, or how learning is to be understood.

In the case of the teacher who is on maternity leave (example 26) and brings up the question whether children need daily morning circle a process of uncovering assumptions is initiated. It stops however once the colleagues leave the school.

The discussion initiated about the school assembly in which the teacher incites a review of the practice against the conceptual ideas (example 34) opens the field for a process of critical investigation. In it the power relations as they are enacted are explicitly named. How far an investigation will follow is open due to the pending process.

In the discussions about saying grace before meals (example 35), the pre-school children to be kept at morning-circle (example 27), and about the obligatory singing during morning circle (example 28) the power relations are explicitly named. In these discussions the legitimacy of adult authority is discussed.

*

For teachers asking critical questions in reflection processes on rituals in schools there is a connection to a critical attitude being present. In this context I want to briefly go back to the example of the teacher who asks her colleagues in the sectional staff meeting about the morning-circle in which a child tells stories about watching television (example 33). We remember this teacher being in her first year after finishing teacher training. Her question asked in the staff meeting about the legitimacy of her prohibiting talk about television in morning circle is triggered by a tender doubt.

She sees a contradiction in asking children for their weekend experiences and at the same time censoring out what a particular child has to say. She herself holds a certain value system (and theory of childhood) in which there is no appreciation of children watching television, and particularly not Star-Wars.

"A – (...) after the weekend, when he tells his story, what he did (...) and that was in fact, ahm, nothing special at all, he had simply watched television. That in itself is bad enough, for a child to only watch television at weekends. But then, not only can he tell you the entire story of the film, he can actually act it out, too.

Q – It seems that was an exciting film.

A – That was Star-Wars. Fourth (...) I can only say, fourth class. Now, I find Star-Wars is not really appropriate for fourth class. On top of it."

Her question is not driven by an anti-authoritarian agenda or impulse. In her entire interview there is no sign of such an agenda. Yet the question as posed has a critical potential. But this potential is not developed at all in the situation where she reflects with her colleagues. She gets an answer to her question that wipes away any trace of a doubt that she had. One may see it as her personal fate that she is paired with those particular colleagues at this particular school. In another school with another parallel class teacher her doubts may have been cultivated by a feedback that would have turned the question into a critical question. Had she by accident been paired with a teacher who holds a critical attitude, the potential of the question could have been actualised. Here it was not.

Which raises the question of the chances of critical questions being asked in an environment where there are no teachers who hold a critical attitude. We remember the example of the teacher who reduces dictation to one per semester. She also reported about 20 years of agony with her former colleague with whom there was no common ground for even scrutinizing the learning theories that inform the practice. It is only when two new colleagues come to the school that she sees an opening.

For critical investigations about rituals to happen in reflection processes of teachers it is obviously necessary also that there is a critical mass, a sufficient number of teachers in a given school who share the desire to investigate power relations and uncover hegemonic assumptions. This is very much common sense. What actually constitutes a sufficient number may differ from one case to another. At any rate the lack of support as a decisive factor in preventing critical reflection to happen is clearly mirrored also in suggestions as made by Sabine Knauer or Stephen Brookfield that it is crucial for teachers to "find a small group of peers – even one person will do – who share your conviction" (Brookfield 1995, p. 239) or to "first encourage small, informal group meetings with colleagues" (Knauer 2006, p. 255).

At the same time that is not to say that critical questions *can not* be asked without such a critical mass. There is no doubt, a teacher can always ask whatever question she or he wants to ask. But for the one who asks the critical question in a situation where there is not sufficient support such a move bears the risk depicted by Stephen Brookfield: "Teachers (...) can commit cultural suicide without even being aware of what they're doing. As they speak about how they're questioning and re-evaluating their practice or how they're doing things differently these days, they run the risk that colleagues will see them as engaged in an act of betrayal. They are whistle-blowers on the culture of stasis – the collective agreement not to rock the boat by asking awkward questions or doing things differently" (Brookfield 1995, p. 236).

Even for those teachers who hold a critical attitude it is a necessity to anticipate the potential risk that comes with asking critical questions. That is why critical questions are more likely to be asked in free alternative schools. There is a critical mass of teachers (and parents) already who have an agenda in line with Foucault's questions: "How not to be governed *like that,* by that, in the name of those principles, with such and such objectives in mind and by means of such procedures, not like that, not for that, not by them" (Foucault 1997, p. 44).

We remember the perspective of investigation as derived from Catherine Bell's argumentation leading to question being asked of actors, not of acts. Therefore Foucault's question for teachers would have to be turned into: How not *govern* like that, by that, in the name of those principles, with such and such objectives in mind and by means of such procedures, not like that, not for that. And the very last part of the quote however would have to read: not by me, not by us.

That is why if critical questions are asked in reflection processes of teachers on rituals in school they are not in fact asked of ritual. The critical question asks about the actors. How reasonable, grounded, explicable is their acting? It asks about their being governors. It asks about their governing in its ambiguity within a wider social context and the legitimacy of acting in just this manner and not in another one.

(Not only) for teachers reflecting on rituals in education these are exactly the questions they would have to engage with if they wanted to come to a conscious practice. What such engagement brings on the plate are inevitably also questions for articulated alternatives. What other options does one have to act?

Outlook: Consciously Enacting Alternatives

In the section on lining up and circle time a snapshot was presented of a development of ritual practices within the dynamics of schools and pedagogic discourse. Obviously there are numerous other practices that would be suited for a similar analysis. For anyone to engage in a critical investigation of school practices it is helpful to have at hand tools that allow to overcome a certain speechlessness when it comes to those practices that take place "specifically in lieu of explicit logical speculation," and are "simultaneously the avoidance of explicit speech and narrative" (Bell 1992, p. 111).

The contributions in this book provide an impression of what is in the tool-box of ritual analysis in education. The comprehensive overview on the theories of ritual in education can be used as an entry portal for a discussion of concrete practices in schools. Approaching these practices as rituals opens dimensions for reflection that otherwise are not accessible in similar fashion.

It is also clear that the theoretical models of reflection that are available so far do not sufficiently represent reflection processes in the professional context of teachers. The suggestion to look at reflection as a social act offers a substantial alternative. The extensive coverage given to the examples in chapter five shows how this approach leads to the detection of a number of re-occurring themes in the professional reflection processes of teachers. What is provided here is also a way of speaking about one's reflective practice that has not been available yet.

Obviously the reflective practices of teachers always revert back to their teaching practices. Reflecting on them is not an end in itself. Reflection is an act that connects two acts. Hence it is related to practice before and practice after. Teachers who are open to a critical investigation of their own ritual practices will therefore be always confronted with the question for practical alternatives. Here it is helpful if articulated alternatives are actually documented and made accessible.

From the perspective of teachers in mainstream schools the free alternative schools can be seen as an articulated alternative. On an international plane there are numerous schools that are committed to principles of self-regulation, or radical democracy. In recent years organisations like International Democratic Education Network (IDEN) or the European Democratic Education Community (EUDEC) have added an organisational dimension to these schools that spans over continents.

It should be remembered that free alternative schools are not free of ritual practices either. In each and every one of them there are ritual practices that are as much “part and parcel” of the interaction system. For the actors in free alternative schools it is similarly necessary to be wary of these elements of their practice. Given the specific ambition in free alternative schools to live according to the principles of personal responsibility and democracy this could be seen as even more important than in mainstream schools. In schools that seek to offer children, teachers and parents the opportunity to practice self-regulation and democracy again and again in everyday life everyone needs to be highly vigilant in monitoring the concrete practices that creep in over time.

The programmatic statements in conceptual papers and theses declarations are one thing. Real life is another one. Teachers, children, parents in free alternative schools do not live in a social vacuum, or an enclave that has no connection to the outer world. Nobody in these schools can claim to be free of influences from wider society. These influences interfere in many ways with the stated aims in free alternative schools, and it is most likely that such influences are acted out in processes of ritualisation. Paper is patient. It is easy to put down a collection of theses in favour of radical democratic principles. It is much harder to make them material reality in the concrete relationships in every day school life.

Hence closely monitoring ritual practices for actors in free alternative schools can be a means to check on the own ambitions against their concrete realisation. Such monitoring requires that practices are consciously subjected to scrutinisation via deliberate rationality.

Within any social setting changes in ritual practices happen constantly via mimetic processes. That is also true for educational institutions. Strategic interventions in negotiations of power relations in form of ritualisation, avoiding explicit speech and narrative, are ongoing at all times. They can be moved on by pupils and teachers alike, sometimes by parents, by principals, simply by anyone who is physically in the field. Any of those moves brings about changes.

But alternatives can and should be more than changes happening in lieu of explicit logical speculation. Critically thinking about rituals in school will inevitably lead into thinking about the institutional character of school, its historic roots and trajectories, its current position in society.

Teachers find themselves in a pivotal position in the institution. Their practice is essential to making school real. Accepting critical questions about their acting in ritualised practices in schools and searching for answers will open the route for changes that are consciously enacted.

Appendix: The Traffic Light System

The ideas of 'traffic lights' or variations thereof as a means of classroom management are virulently spread amongst teachers. In the interviews teachers from German mainstream and Irish primary schools made reference to their use. An example:

A – I have introduced these cards, green, yellow and red cards, ahm, which the children get when they work. And that goes in both directions. They get a green card if it works well. It can turn to a yellow one if it it is not so, but they can also get the green one back. Back and forth, I would say, in both directions.

Q – Could you explain to me, what exactly you do with these cards?

A – Well, I have a set of cards. And when the children work, or also at circle time, at circle time I show them, ahm. Because I found that when I tell off a child that is, I would say, a bit like stored somewhere. But if the child has a green, yellow or red card lying on the desk (...) then it is visually in sight for the child.

Q – Let us take a situation, a lesson (...) the children sit there everywhere.

A – Exactly, the children sit at their desk, and I give them a task. They start working. (...) And then there are children who sit and work silently with a partner, or on their own, whatever, they work. And then I put a green card down.

Q – While they are working?

A – While they are working.

(...)

A – Then there are children, who sit at the sides, ahm, I don't know, or shout, well, I have, I have a couple of children in this class who on principle shout through the class. (...) They get, like, a yellow card put down.

Q – Yes, and what do they do then?

A – Then they are quiet and try to contain themselves, most of them. Obviously sometimes it also fails, but most of them really get it, that they say, O.K., 'uuuh, now I have yellow, I am going to work better.' (...) Then they get a green one again.

Q – How many children are in that class?

A – Twenty.

Q – O.K., now :

A – Do you say, how to organise? [laughs]

Q – Yes, how then do you get [laughing: all these cards out there? I mean /]

A – That works well. It does not work well at all times, but usually, ahm, once they have a green card, they want to keep it, too.

Q – Well, does that really mean, I find it fascinating, does it really mean, all twenty children have a card lying in front of them.

A – Mhmh. Then at the end of the lesson they enter into a list, that is how I do it in my own class, in the other class I do it for them, ahm, and that works. And then they are like, they want to collect as many greed cards during the week as possible.

Q – They collect them, yes, O.K. And you said, there are red cards also. What are they for?

A – Well, red is then, on the card it says: time-thieve. These then are those children, where it simply didn't work at all. And with these children I have a chat, and, ahm, see, how can we improve this, that it works better. And that can be then that I, ahm, give the child a task: 'Now you please write a report, what happened today, how did you behave wrongly.' As in, where the children basically are supposed to reflect upon their behaviour again.

Q – Mhmh.

A – Ahm, and depending on the child, sometimes I also say: 'Please, parents signature.' Ahm, yes, and mostly that works well again, too. And if not, I will go to talk to the parents again.

Literature

Althans, Birgit / Göhlich, Michael (2004); *"Rituelles Wissen and organisatorisches Lernen"* in: Zeitschrift für Erziehungswissenschaft, Beiheft 2-04, Innovation und Ritual, Wiesbaden; pp. 206 – 221

Althans, Birgit / Tull, Marc; (2013); *"Irritations of School Routines and Institutional Diversification of Care-Services in Primary Education – A Multidimensional Access to Food-Services in Allday-Schools"* Paper presented to the Ethnography and Education Conference, Oxford, September 2013

Audehm, Kathrin (2004); *"Ritual – Sprache – Körper"* in: Zeitschrift für Erziehungswissenschaft, Beiheft 2-04, Innovation und Ritual, Wiesbaden; pp. 46 – 57

Baader, Meike S. (2008); *"Öffentliche Kleinkinderziehung in Deutschland im Fokus des Politischen. Von den Kindergärten 1848 zu den Kinderläden der 68er Bewegung"* in: Ecarius, Jutta / Groppe, Carola / Malmede, Hans (Ed.) (2008): *Familie und öffentliche Erziehung. Theoretische Konzeptionen, historische und aktuelle Analysen.* Wiesbaden; pp. 267 - 289

Bell, Catherine (1992); *Ritual theory – Ritual practice;* New York/Oxford

Bell, Catherine (1997); *Ritual - Perspectives and Dimensions*; New York/Oxford

Bellenberg, Gabriele / Hovestadt, Gertrud / Klemm, Klaus (unter Mitarbeit von Nicole Keßler, Eva Museller, Katrin Rudolph, Anja Tummes) (2004); *Selektivität und Durchlässigkeit im allgemein bildenden Schulsystem. Rechtliche Regelungen und Daten unter besonderer Berücksichtigung der Gleichwertigkeit von Abschlüssen;* Essen

Bernfeld, Siegfried (1973, orig. 1925); *Sisyphus or The limits of Education*; Berkeley – Original edition: *Sisiphos – Die Grenzen der Erziehung*; Vienna

Bernstein, Basil (1964); *"Elaborated and Restricted Codes: Their Social Origins and Some Consequences"* in: American Anthropologist, New Series, Vol. 66, No. 6, Part 2: The Ethnography of Communication, pp. 55-69

Bernstein, Basil (2003, orig.1975); *Class, Codes and Control: Vol. III Towards a theory of educational transmission,* Abington/New York, 2003

Bernstein, Basil / Elvin Lionel H. / Peters Richard S. (1975, orig. 1971); *"Ritual in Education"* in: *School and Society – a sociological reader;* London; pp. 160 -165; First in: *Philosophical Transactions of the Royal Society of London* (1966)

BFAS (Ed.) (1992); *Freie Alternativschulen: Kinder machen Schule. Innen- und Außenansichten;* Wolfratshausen

BFAS (2012); http://www.freie-alternativschulen.de

Bildungskommission NRW (1995); *Zukunft der Bildung, Schule der Zukunft;* Neuwied, Kriftel, Berlin

Blanford, Roxanne (2009); *Paul Watzlawick's Second Axiom of Communication;* source: http://suite101.com/article/paul-watzlawicks-second-axiom-of-communication-a162645

Boehme, Jeanette (2004); *"Die mythische Dimension in schulischen Ritualen: Rekonstruktion und Theoretisierung einer gescheiterten Performance"* in: Zeitschrift für Erziehungswissenschaft, Beiheft 2-04, Innovation und Ritual, Wiesbaden; pp. 231 – 250

Bohnsack, Ralf (2004); *"Rituale des Aktionismus bei Jugendlichen"* in: Zeitschrift für Erziehungswissenschaft, Beiheft 2-04, Innovation und Ritual, Wiesbaden; pp. 81 – 90

Borchert, Manfred (1992); *"Zur aktuellen Lage der Freien Alternativschulen in Deutschland"* in: BFAS (Ed.); *Freie Alternativschulen: Kinder machen Schule. Innen- und Außenansichten; Wolfratshausen*; Wolfrathshausen; pp. 15 - 23

Borchert, Manfred (1995); *"Was unterscheidet Freie Alternativschulen von anderen"* in: Borchert, Manfred / Maas, Michael; *Freie Alternativschulen : die Zukunft der Schule hat schon begonnen*; Bad Heilbrunn; pp. 36 - 82

Brookfield, Stephen (1985); *"Community Adult Education: A Comparative Analysis of Theory and Practice"* in: Comparative Education Review, Vol. 29, No. 2; pp. 232-239

Brookfield, Stephen (1995); *Becoming a critically reflective teacher;* San Francisco

Brookfield, Stephen (2010); *"Critical Reflection as an adult learning process"* in: Nona Lyons (Ed.); *Handbook of Reflection and Reflective Inquiry: Mapping a Way of Knowing for Professional Reflective Inquiry*; New York; pp. 215 – 236

Burningham,John (1987); *John Patrick Norman McHennessy, the boy who was always late*; London

Bushnell, Mary (1997); *"Small school ritual and parent involvement"* in: The Urban Review, Vol. 29, No. 4; pp. 283 – 295

Büttner, Manfred (1996); *"Stille-Übungen mit dem Regenstabzauber"* in: pt-intern, Nr. 39

Collins, Bernie (2011); *Empowering Children through Circle Time: An illumination of Practice*; Doctoral thesis NUI Maynooth

Collins, Randall (2004) ; *Interaction Ritual Chains;* Princeton

Combe, Arno (2000); *"Wie tragfähig ist der Rekurs auf Rituale"* in: Annemarie von der Groeben (Ed.) (2000); Hamburg; pp. 105 - 111

Daublebsky , Benita / Lauble , Silvia (unter Mitarbeit von: Susanne Frank) (2006); *Eine Handreichung für die Praxis . Der Klassenrat als Mittel demokratischer Schulentwicklung* . Berlin

Denscombe, Martyn (1985); *Classroom Control, A Sociological Perspective;* London

DES (Department of Education and Skills) (2012); *The Forum on Patronage and Pluralism in the Primary Sector. Report of the Forum's Advisory Group;* Dublin

Dewey, John (2007, orig. 1910); *How we think*; Stilwell

die tageszeitung 29. 01. 2003

Drudy, Sheelagh / Lynch, Kathleen (1993); *Schools and Society in Ireland;* Dublin

Dücker, Burckhard (2007); *Rituale. Formen – Funktionen – Geschichte;* Stuttgart/Weimar

Dücker, Burckhard (2012); *"Rituale"* in: Erwägen, Wissen, Ethik; Vol. 23, No. 2; pp. 165 - 173

Durkheim, Emile (1947); *The elementary forms of the religious life: A study in religious sociology;* The Free Press, Glencoe, Illinois (first published 1915); translated by Joseph W. Swain

Eckstein, Andreas (2000); *"Rituale (ver)wenden"* in: Annemarie von der Groeben (Ed.) (2000); Hamburg; pp. 49 – 58

EKD (Ed.) 2008; *Schulen in evangelischer Trägerschaft. Selbstverständnis, Leistungsfähigkeit, Perspektiven;* Gütersloh/München

Eltern-Kind-Initiative e. V. (1997); *Konzept für eine Freie Schule in Seligenstadt;* Seligenstadt

Erikson, Erik H. (1950), *Childhood and society,* New York, 1950

Erikson, Erik H. (1966); *"Ontogeny of ritualisation"* in: Loewenstein/Newman/Schur/Solnit (Eds.); *Psychoanalysis – a general psychology,* New York; pp. 601 - 622

Fend, Helmut (1980); *Theorie der Schule*; München-Wien-Baltimore

F.I.P.P. (1982); *Rechtshandbuch für Erzieher/innen am Beispiel Berlin;* Berlin

Foucault, Michel (1982); *"The subject and power"* in: Critical Inquiry, Vol. 8, No. 4; pp. 777 - 795

Foucualt, Michel (1995, orig. 1977); *Discipline and Punish;* New York

Foucault, Michel (1996); *Foucault live. Collected Interviews, 1961 – 1984;* New York

Foucault, Michel (1997); *"What is critique"* in: Foucault, Michel; *The Politics of Truth*; Los Angeles; pp. 41 - 81

Freies Lernen in Berlin e. V. (Ed.) (2011); *Freie Schule am Mauerpark. Von der Idee zur Wirklichkeit;* Berlin

Fürstenau, Peter (1969); *"Zur Psychoanalyse der Schule als Institution"* in: Pädagogisches Zentrum; *Zur Theorie der Schule;* Weinheim/Berlin/Basel; pp. 47 - 66

Gehrke, Nathalie J. (1979); *"Rituals of the hidden curriculum"* in: Kaora Yamamoto (Ed.) *Children in time and space*, New York/London; pp. 103 - 177

Goffman, Erving (1968); *Asylums;* Baltimore 1968

Göhlich, Michael (2004); *"Rituale und Schule"* in: Zeitschrift für Erziehungswissenschaft, Beiheft 2-04, Innovation und Ritual; Wiesbaden; pp. 17 – 28

Gore, Joanna Stephanie (2004); *Leave me alone;* London

Gribble, David (2012); *Democratic Decision-making;* source: http://www.davidgribble.co.uk/democratic-decision-making.htm

Griffiths, Morwenna / Tann, Sarah (1992); *"Using reflective practice to link personal and public theories"* in: Journal of Education for teaching; *18* (1); pp. 69 – 84

Habermas, Jürgen (1968); Erkenntnis und Interesse; Frankfurt/M.

Hamm, Robert (1999); *Tanz nicht aus der Reihe;* Langen

Hartlaub, Marei (2004); *Konzept der Freien Schule Frankfurt;* Frankfurt/M.

Hartlaub, Michael / Stubenrauch, Renate (1977); *"Ansätze und Schwierigkeiten einer politischen Strategie zur Veränderung der Grundschule"* in: Seifert, Monika/Nagel Herbert (Ed.) 1977; *Nicht für die Schule leben. Ein alternativer Schulversuch. Freie Schule Frankfurt;* Frankfurt/M.; pp. 50 - 57

Hatton, Neville/Smith, David (1995); *"Reflection in Teacher Education: Towards Definition and Implementation"* in: Teaching & Teacher Education, Vol. 11, No. 1, pp. 33 - 49

Haug, Frigga (1999); *Vorlesungen zur Einführung in die Erinnerungsarbeit – The Duke Lectures;* Hamburg;

Henry, Mary E. (1993); *School Cultures – universes of meaning in private schools*, Norwood NJ

Hessisches Schulgesetz in der Fassung vom 14. Juni 2005 (GVBl. I S. 441), zuletzt geändert durch Gesetz vom 21. November 2011 (GVBl. I S. 679) , Wiesbaden

Hinz, Alfred (2000); *"Schulkultur ist Lebenskultur"* in: Annemarie von der Groeben (Ed.) (2000); Hamburg; pp. 75 – 83

HKWM (2011); Verordnung zur Ausgestaltung der Bildungsgänge und Schulformen der Grundstufe (Primarstufe) und der Mittelstufe (Sekundarstufe I) und der Abschlussprüfungen in der Mittelstufe (VOBGM)

Vom 14. Juni 2005 (ABl. S. 438; ber. S. 579), zuletzt geändert durch Verordnung vom 19. August 2011 (ABl. S. 582)

IDEN (2005); Declaration of the International Democratic Education Conference, held in Berlin 2005; http://www.idenetwork.org

INTO (2010); *Assessment in the Primary School Discussion Document and Proceedings of the Consultative Conference on Education 2008 ;* Dublin

Jones, Alison (Ed.) (2001); *Touchy Subjects, Teachers touching children;* Dunedin, NZ

Kapferer, Judith L. (1981); *"Socialisation and the Symbolic Order of the School"* in: Anthropology & Education Quarterly, Vol 12, No. 4; pp. 258 – 274

Katz, Steven / Dack, Lisa / Earl, Lorna (2009); *"Networked learning communities. Fostering Learning for Teachers and the Students"* in: Principal Connections, Vol. 12, Issue 3; pp. 36 - 38

Kellermann, Ingrid (2008); *Vom Kind zum Schulkind,* Opladen & Farmington Hills

Knauer, Sabine (2006); *"Zur (Wieder-)Entdeckung der Lehrkräfte als Subjekte – Ein subjektiv-wissenschaftliches Plädoyer für einen Tabubruch"* in: Rihm, Thomas; *Schulentwicklung. Vom Subjektstandpunkt ausgehen ...;* Wiesbaden; pp. 241 - 256

Kvale, Steinar (2011; orig. 2007); *Doing Interviews;* London

Langer, Anje (2008); *Disziplinieren und Entspannen*; Bielefeld

Lin, Xiaodong / Schwartz, Daniel (2003); *"Reflection at the Crosroads of Cultures"* in: Mind, Culture and Activity 10(1); pp. 9 - 25

Lortie, Dan. C. (1964); *The teacher and team teaching: suggestions for long-range research;* in: J. T. Shaplin and H. F. Olds, jun. (eds.); *Teach Teaching*; New York. Quoted in: Denscombe (1985), p 70

Maas, Michael (1995); *"Geschichte, Mythen und Erfolge der Alternativschulbewegung"* in: Borchert, Manfred / Maas, Michael (1995); *Freie Alternativschulen : die Zukunft der Schule hat schon begonnen*; Bad Heilbrunn; pp. 15 - 35

Mannheim, Karl (1982); *Structures of Thinking;* London

McLaren, Peter (1986); *Schooling as a ritual performance;* London

McLoughlin, Owen (2005); *"Citizen Child – the experience of a student council in a primary school"* in: INTO (2010)

Mezirow, Jack (1991); *Transformative Dimensions of Adult Learning;* San Francisco, 1991

Mosley, Jenny (2004); *Turn your school around;* Cambridge

Münte-Goussar , Stephan (2001); *Selbst-Sein. Zur Gouvernementalität der humanen und autonomen Schule;* Hamburg

Nagel, Herbert (1977); *"Die pädagogische Illusion"* in: Seifert, Monika / Nagel Herbert (Ed.) (1977); Frankfurt/M.; pp. 116 - 128

NCCA, National Council for Curriculum and Assessment (2008); Primary Curriculum Review Phase 2; Dublin

Neill, Alexander Sutherland (1982); *das prinzip summerhill: fragen und antworten;* Hamburg

Ovens, Alan / Tinning, Richard (2009); *"Reflection as situated practice: A memory-work study of lived experience in teacher education"* in: Teaching and Teacher Education 25 (2009); pp. 1125 - 1131

Piper, Hauke (1997), *"Das Ritual als inszenierte Widersprüchlichkeit"* in: Hanna Kiper, *Selbst- und Mitbestimmung in der Schule: das Beispiel Klassenrat;* Hohengehren; pp. 217 – 242

Prengel, Annedore / Heinzel, Friedericke (2004); *"Anerkennungs- und Missachtungsrituale in schulischen Geschlechterverhältnissen"* in: Zeitschrift für Erziehungswissenschaft, Beiheft 2-04, Innovation und Ritual; Wiesbaden; pp. 115 – 128

Quantz, Richard (1999); *"School ritual as performance: a reconstruction of Durkheim's and Turner's uses of ritual"* in: Educational Theory; Vol. 49 Issue 4; pp. 493 - 513

Quantz, Richard / Magolda, Peter (1997); *"Nonrational classroom performance: Ritual as an aspect of action"* in: The Urban Review, Vol. 29, No. 4; pp. 221 – 238

Reimer, Franz (2010); *"School attendance as a civic duty v. home education as a human right"* in: International Electronic Journal of Elementary Education; Vol. 3, Issue 1

Riegel, Enja (2000); *"Rituale oder: die Kultur des Zusammenleben"* in: Annemarie von der Groeben (Ed.) (2000); Hamburg; pp. 21 – 30

Rodgers, Carol (2010); *"The role of descriptive inquiry in Building Presence and civic capacity"* in: Nona Lyons (Ed.); *Handbook of Reflection and Reflective Inquiry: Mapping a Way of Knowing for Professional Reflective Inquiry*; New York, pp. 45 – 61

Sattler, Stephan (2007); *Rituale im Grundschulunterricht;* Landau

Schäfer, Alfred (2004); *"Differenzerzeugung und Macht"* in: Zeitschrift für Erziehungswissenschaft, Beiheft 2-04, *Innovation und Ritual*, Wiesbaden; pp. 222 – 230

Scholz, Gerold (1996); *Kinder lernen von Kindern;* Baltmannsweiler

Seifert, Monika (1969); *Zur Theorie der antiautoritären Kindergärten;* in: Konkret 3/1969, reprint in: Seifert/Nagel (1977), pp 11 - 15

Seifert, Monika / Nagel Herbert (Ed.) (1977); *Nicht für die Schule leben. Ein alternativer Schulversuch. Freie Schule Frankfurt;* Frankfurt/M.

Steffensky, Fulbert (2000); *"Rituale als Lebensinszenierungen"* in: Annemarie von der Groeben (Ed.) (2000); pp. 97 – 104

Stubenrauch, Renate (1992); *"Danke, Renne, es hat Spaß gemacht"* in: BFAS (Ed.) (1992); Wolfratshausen; pp. 26 – 38

SZ (30. 10. 2012); Süddeutsche Zeitung; *Durchlässigkeit im deutschen Schulsystem – Mehr Absteiger als Aufsteiger*; http://sz.de/1.1510055

Von der Groeben, Annemarie (Ed.) (2000); *Rituale in Schule und Unterricht,* Hamburg

Wagner-Willi, Monika (2005); *Kinder-Rituale zwischen Vorder- und Hinterbühne.* Wiesbaden

Waller, Willard W. (1932); *The sociology of teaching;* New York

Watzlawick, Paul / Beavin, Janet / Jackson, Don (1967); *Pragmatics of human communication: A study of interactional patterns, pathologies, and paradoxes.* New York

Wellendorf, Franz (1979, orig. 1973); *Schulische Sozialisation und Identität*, Weinheim

Wellendorf, Franz (2011) – Interview held on 10. 3. 2011

Winkler, Ameli (1994); *"Rituale in der Grundschule – Erfundende Wirklichkeiten gestalten"* in: Pädagogik Heft 1/94 Titelthema: *Rituale – Schule und Unterricht Gestalt geben*, Weinheim; pp. 67 – 74

Wulf, Christoph (2004); *"Die innovative Kraft von Ritualen in der Erziehung"* in: Zeitschrift für Erziehungswissenschaft, Beiheft 2-04, Innovation und Ritual, Wiesbaden; pp. 9 – 16

Wulf, Christoph (2006); *"Towards a historico-cultural anthropology of education"* in: Tobias Werler/Christoph Wulf (Eds.); *Hidden Dimensions of Education;* Münster; pp. 199 – 207

Wulf, Christoph / Althans, Birgit / Audehm, Kathrin / Bausch, Constanze / Göhlich, Michael / Sting, Stephan / Tervooren, Anja / Wagner-Willi, Monika / Zirfaß, Jörg (2010); *Ritual and Identity;* London

Wulf, Christoph / Althans, Birgit / Audehm, Kathrin / Blaschke, Gerald / Ferrin, Nino / Kellermann, Ingrid / Mattig, Ruprecht / Schinkel, Sebastian (2011); *Die Geste in Erziehung, Bildung, und Sozialisation;* Wiesbaden

Wulf, Christoph / Zirfaß, Jörg (2004); *"Performative Welten, Einführung in die historischen, systematischen und methodischen Dimensionen des Rituals"* in: Wulf/Zirfaß (Ed.), *Die Kultur des Rituals*, Munich; pp. 7 - 45

Xiao, Jiamei (2008); *Children's experience of the rituals of schooling: a case study.* Doctoral thesis, University of Huddersfield

Zerrenner, Carl C. G. (1826); *Grundsätze der Schul-Disciplin für Schulaufseher, Lehrer und Schullehrer-Seminarien;* Magdeburg

Ziehe, Thomas (1987); *"Für inszenierte Ereignisse und gegen die symbolische Verödung des Schule"* in: Westermann Pädagogische Beiträge 7/8 1987, pp. 16 – 19